DELAWARE PARK

DELAWARE PARK

Winners, Losers and Long Shots

Kenneth Baumgardt

The History Press

Published by The History Press
Charleston, SC 29403
www.historypress.net

Cover design by Marshall Hudson.

Unless otherwise noted, all images are from the Collections of the Christiana Historical Society, Christiana, Delaware.

First published 2008

Manufactured in the United States

ISBN 978.1.59629.466.0

Library of Congress CIP data applied for.

Contents

Preface

This is the story of Delaware Park, a famous horse racing track in Stanton, New Castle County, Delaware. The great names of the thoroughbred industry walked along the tree-lined paddocks—War Admiral, Dauber, Kelso, Afleet Alex, Barbaro, Carl Hanford, Eddie Arcaro, Angel Cordero Jr.—not to mention well-known racing aficionados William duPont Jr., Don Ross, Ed Burke, Bayard Sharp, Jane duPont Lunger and many others. This is their story, their contributions and the ups and downs of a quiet little country racetrack.

This book is the first publication of the Christiana, Delaware Historical Society. Founded in 1968 as a civic association, the Christiana Historical Society collects information on the colonial village of Christiana and the surrounding area. Eventually, we hope to use funds from this book and future works to support a local history museum here to inform and educate the general public about the region's history.

Having grown up next door to Delaware Park, I have many fond memories of the park as a happy part of my childhood. Many times my father would take me to the park on a sunny Saturday afternoon to watch the horses run. I attended the opening ceremonies of the American Freedom Train when it stopped there, and in my later days, when the racetrack was closed and used for hosting flea markets and circuses, I was there for them too. When I began to work in my chosen profession of archaeology, my first summer was spent digging on an ancient Native American site on Delaware Park property.

Delaware Park is one of this area's best-known attractions, especially since the addition of slots gambling there. People from miles away come to play the slots here or to watch the races. The park has had its ups and downs, and is currently threatened by regional gambling competition, but the locals here appreciate the last seventy years of excitement the park has brought to the area.

The genesis of this book was Derby Day, 2006. Excited by the prospects of Barbaro, I was encouraged by a close friend to go to the park and put ten dollars to win on that horse. Even on Simulcast, you could feel the excitement in the air that day for one of our local heroines. Then I donated another ten dollars to the slots parlor. Afterward, walking around the beautiful paddock, I began to ponder about the history of the racetrack.

Although I had grown up only a stone's throw down the street, and had walked these beautiful groves before, I never really had heard much about the track's history or its impact on the local community. When I returned home I searched the Internet to find the official website of the Delaware Park Racetrack, which provided a good overview of the park but left me thirsty for more details. And so the search began...

The Origins of American Horse Racing

God gave us horses because they're the most beautiful creatures on this planet.
—author unknown

Horse racing in America is as old as America itself. America itself was largely built on the backs of horses, and there is little doubt that the love and admiration that the owners had for their animals led to more enjoyable pursuits.

The first known racetrack was built in 1665 on Long Island, New York, at a place called Hempstead Plain.[1] In the early days, large areas of clear land were not available as in England; horse racing instead developed into a short-track form, in which the horses were raced along a roadway to a chosen point, usually a pole marking the spot, and then turned around to return to the finish line.

Even with these relatively primitive conditions, the general rules for horse racing were essentially the same as today. Horses were weighed and adjusted according to age, fillies received an allowance from males and entry fees were waged on the horses before the races. Many of these races were the highlights of county and town fairs, the excitement of these early races giving the colonial settlers and their horses as well a much-needed break from their chores at clearing and planting fields and establishing the communities. The races also brought together horses from distant parts to be traded, sold and mated.

Although flat racing was popular in the Northern states, the first mile-long oval tracks appeared in Virginia. In the Southern states, and to a smaller extent in Maryland, large areas of land were cleared for the planting of tobacco there, allowing for large areas to be outfitted with oval tracks after the crops were harvested. The Virginian planters also maintained stronger ties to the English upper class, and they began to purchase quarter horses from England that were better suited for the rigors of tobacco farming but also better suited to the longer racecourses. This difference from the Northern colonies was the origin of the strong tradition of landed gentry families in the South being associated with racing. An example of this was the Tayloes of Mount Airy, Virginia. John Tayloe II owned the renowned horse Yorick during the Revolutionary War, who was carried from town to town taking on anyone willing to lose to it. Yorick could run a five-mile heat in twelve minutes and twenty-seven seconds.[2]

In Maryland, at least twenty racing centers were established before the Revolutionary War. Early tracks were established at Baltimore and Annapolis. Important for the history of racing in the area was the interests of Governor Benjamin Ogle, who established a stud farm at his estate at Belair. This farm was continuously operated for centuries as a center for breeding, and in the twentieth century was the home of the well-known horses Gallant Fox, Omaha, Flares, Granville, Fenelon and Nashua.[3] Colonel Benjamin Tasker Jr., who owned Belair after Ogle's death, raced Selina in a notable intercolonial race against John Tayloe II in December 1752, netting a $10,000 prize against the Virginian horse.

Like the other colonies, Delaware has always had horse racing in its blood. In 1687, Henry Bowman sued to recover one thousand pounds of tobacco, which he claimed to have won in a horse race. Often people from a region would meet when the county court was in session, to observe or to participate, and it became a venue for impromptu horse racing. "In 1704, the Court at Lewes made an order prohibiting the riding of horses in the town during the sitting of the Court as a great hindrance to the dispatch of business, because of the neglect of the people in attendance to the court."[4] The first formal racing facility in the state was built in the town of Newark in 1760.[5]

According to the Delaware historian Walter A. Powell, writing about the county fairs during the time of the Revolution, "The Delawareans were lovers of fine horses in those days." Horse racing was one of the great "attractions at the Faires." Even the sober minded Quaker entered into the sport. He wrote that a Friend, who afterward became a minister, admitted that he was "frisky in his early years, and acknowledged himself to blame for running at a horse race at Chester faire, and is heartily sorry for it, and hope never to do it again."[6]

Racing was often hosted on the streets of the young state, with the race consisting of a group of horses running down a chosen road, passing around a marked post and then running back to the beginning. An advertisement for such a race held in the village of Christiana Bridge, only two miles from where Delaware Park would be built many years later, was found in 1778.[7] Similar advertisements for horse races in the area at this time were found for Duck Creek (Smyrna) and Middletown, Delaware; East Nottingham (Rising Sun, Maryland), Head of Bohemia and Charlestown, Maryland; and York and Chester, Pennsylvania.

Although a long tradition of racing horses was well established in colonial America, the forces that formed the nation had a negative effect on the industry. The new ethics of the Revolutionary era, largely based upon Quaker religious traditions, saw racing, gambling, drinking to excess and smoking as social ills that did not fit well into the morals of a new society built upon lofty goals of equality and temperance. Public outcry soon after the Revolution led to the abolishment of horse racing in many areas. In 1792, the Virginia Assembly passed a law prohibiting all bets of more than seven dollars at "any horse race, cock fighting, or any other sport or pastime."[8] Soon afterward, similar laws were passed in the Quaker havens of New York, Pennsylvania and New Jersey. In Delaware, although the new capital of the state was in rural Dover, the political and moral power base was in New Castle County, which was strongly influenced by Quaker moralists from Philadelphia. Horse racing was one of the ills of society that were outlawed. Governor Joshua Clayton, the first elected governor of Delaware, acted in his first year in office in 1789 to outlaw "horseracing, foot-racing, cock-fighting and shooting-matches," due to the fact that these activities attracted people who drank too much.[9]

This change in attitude only resulted in a stronger development of horse racing in the Southern states like Kentucky, Tennessee and Virginia, which continued to maintain stronger ties with English aristocracy during the early nineteenth century and developed the breeding stocks that would result in the thoroughbred horses.

Thus began an era of prohibition against horse racing in Delaware, which would last for a total of 147 years. Even with the prohibition against gambling, horse racing continued in the nineteenth century around Delaware. County fairs perpetuated the sport until the Depression era after World War I. Although betting was not allowed, private wagers among gentlemen were made. Scheutzen Park featured meets in the 1870s, and Hazel Dell Park ran races for three years in Wilmington, from 1888 to 1890.[10] There is little doubt that betting was done at these races, although covertly.

Sulky races were a favorite sport at the former Wawaset Driving Park, the area of west Wilmington bounded by Pennsylvania, Greenhill and Woodlawn Avenues and Seventh Street. Until 1917, Wawaset Park was the site of the Delaware State Fair. Some of the

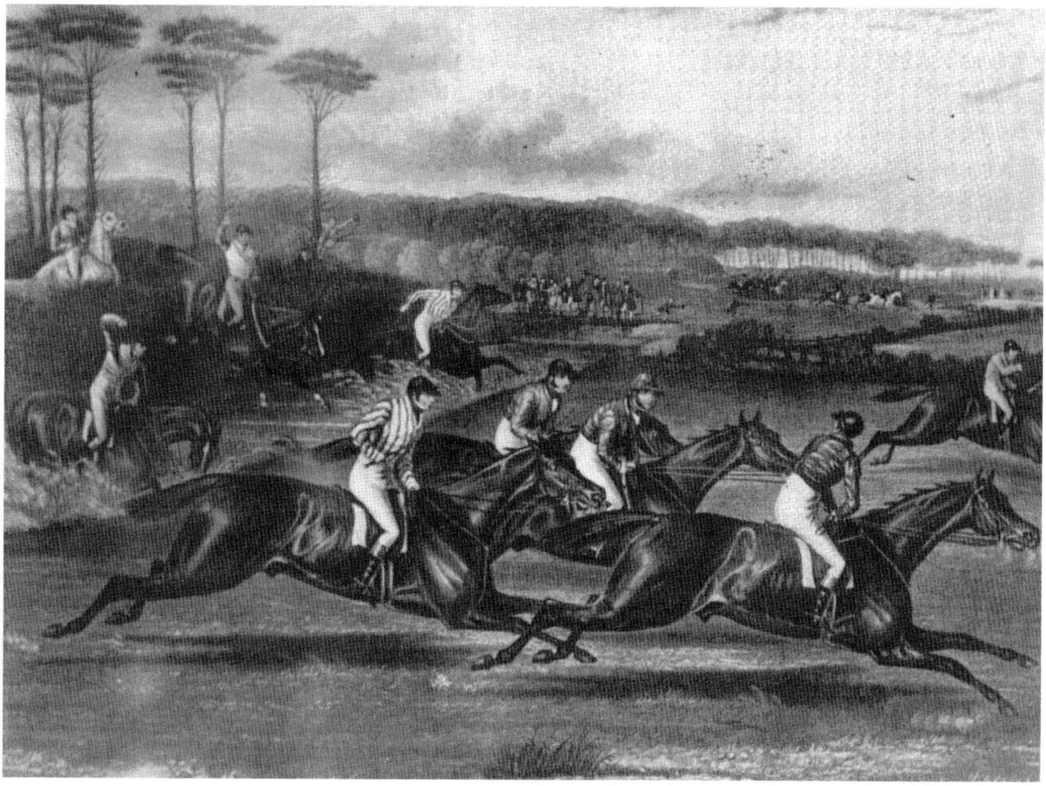

Leamingtoin Grand Steeplechase, 1837. *From* Steeplechasing, *Thayer, 1949.*

finest harness racing was conducted at Wawaset, according to George J. Bacon, owner of the famous Gay Harry, who in 1925 was the only living stallion in the country that could date back four times to Hambletonian 10 (1849–1876), from whose four sons the lineage of virtually all American Standardbred race horses can be traced.

These races ran without interruption from 1910 until the beginning of World War I in 1917, attracting weekly crowds of up to five thousand. Among the leading owners were the late Senator T. Coleman DuPont, whose Little Lady turned the mile in 2.08¾; John J. Jones, who owned Jack Dillman; Joe Maleista; James P. Winchester; and Thomas Lynch. Jones's outstanding racer was Jack Dillman, while Miss Jefferson was the pride of the Winchester fleet. Although the crowds loved having the state fair close to the populated area of the state, the westward expansion of the city of Wilmington eventually forced Wawaset Park out of business.[11]

The races were later moved to the new Kent-Sussex Fairground in Harrington. The idea for the Harrington Fair had been born in 1919, but it wasn't until 1920 that the Kent and Sussex County Fair was incorporated. The original purpose of the corporation was "to have or manage a fair or exposition for the purpose of promoting and encouraging Agriculture and of giving pleasures and diversions to the inhabitants of rural communities within the State of Delaware." Although it was originally conceived as a downstate fair, with the closure of Wawaset Park the fair became known as the Delaware State Fair. Thirty acres were purchased and the first fair was held there on July 27, 1920. Even in this earliest of all state fairs, harness racing was one of the main attractions, as it continues to the present.[12] Until the end of the Depression, the Delaware State Fair was the closest that Delawareans could get to horse racing.

Thoroughbred racing history in the Eastern United States dates to 1864, when Saratoga was constructed in Upstate New York. The second major track was the Pimlico Race Course, near Baltimore, built in 1870. Going to the horse races there became a major form of entertainment for the people of Baltimore during the late 1900s.

In 1910 there arose an anti-gambling movement that resulted in the prohibition of the sport everywhere across the country, except for Maryland and Kentucky. Horse racing was plagued by fraud. The odds and the payouts were often faked, and the bookmakers often owned the horses as well and could influence the races to their favor. "Ringers," fraudulent substitutes that could run faster or slower than the entrant horse could, also were common to throw the races.

A Victorian morality led to the abandonment of virtually all forms of gambling. Arizona and New Mexico were forced to outlaw casinos as a condition of them receiving statehood. Pimlico's Billy Riggs pioneered the use of "French-pools," or parimutuel machines, which were less controversial than bookmakers and allowed the sport to continue.[13] Nonetheless, during the Depression only a few of the racetracks in the Eastern United States were allowed to operate.

During World War I, America became gripped in horse racing fever, due to the success of one special horse. Man o' War, perhaps the best-known name in horse racing history, was born in Lexington, Kentucky, on March 29, 1917, at Nursery Stud Farm. The spawn of Fair Plan and Mahubah, he won his first race at Belmont Park on June 6, 1919. Man o' War went on to win twenty of his twenty-one races, and $249,465 in purses. The horse was such a phenomenon that the country wanted more racing available to them.

At the height of the Depression, attempts were made to end the prohibition on horse racing and efforts began to change the laws in Delaware to permit horse racing there. It was Man o' War's legacy as a stud that had a major impact on racing during the 1930s. His offspring resulted in sixty-four stakes winners and two hundred various champions. Among the notable horses that were born to him were America Flag, Crusader, Battleship and 1937 Triple Crown winner War Admiral. Another offspring, Hard Tack, sired Seabiscuit, which subsequently sired War Relic. Most of the early thoroughbreds in American racing were close descendants of Man o' War.

Willie Built the Joint

With easy seat behold them ride—
These are the truly qualified—
Models of Sporting Men;
Graceful and elegant, yet neat;
Egad, the very sight's a treat
I long to have again!
—author unknown

After more than a century of prohibition against gambling and horse racing in Delaware, the puritanical ideals were well established in the society, and it would take someone of courage and conviction to change the minds of the people. That person was William DuPont Jr., a member of a family that was synonymous with northern Delaware, the finer things of life and a love for the entire spectrum of the horse.

The first inklings of change came near the end of the Roaring Twenties, an era destined to try to break long-standing traditions, enjoy the fast pace of technological innovation and relish in the carefree time of fun and lightness after the horrors of the Great War. Horse racing and parimutuel wagering began to make a comeback. In 1933, Michigan, New Hampshire, Ohio and California legalized parimutuel betting. The California Legislature adopted a statute in 1933 referred to as the Horse Racing Act. The statutes took effect upon adoption by the voters of an amendment to the constitution in June of 1933. The financial difficulties in the Depression forced the change in attitudes nationwide. In 1933, Texas repealed laws against betting, and soon afterward a man received a license to build a cat racing track in Mesquite, Texas.[14] During the 1930s, twenty-one states brought back racetracks. New laws and automated systems made horse racing much more honest than during the 1800s.

Modern horse racing in Delaware traces its roots to the town of Elsmere, just south of Wilmington. The Elsmere Exhibitor's & Breeders Association scheduled a fifteen-day meet at the Elsmere Fair Grounds in June of 1928, but the effort was discontinued after the second day when the attorney general's office ruled the donation system being used was a thinly disguised attempt at gambling, and thus was against the existing state law.

Before the decision was made to close the affair, seven races were run over the half-mile track on both days that the track operated.

The successful rebirth of racing in Delaware is attributed to the efforts of a single individual. William "Willie" DuPont Jr., son of the famous industrial family in Delaware that had a keen interest in the sporting fields of racing and fox hunting, used his influence to see the laws changed. He also built the racecourses and supported the infrastructure necessary for the successful development of the industry.

Horse racing opportunities near Delaware were also limited. Pimlico in Baltimore had been racing since 1870 and the Aqueduct in New York was established in 1894, but the closest racing venue to Delawareans was at Havre de Grace, Maryland. This small course was built in 1912, and although it saw the likes of Man o' War run at it, the facility wasn't designed according to modern racing standards. What Delaware needed was its own, modern course and an integrated system of thoroughbred racing throughout the middle Atlantic, and it took someone like William DuPont to have the power and prestige to make it happen.

William DuPont Jr. was born February 11, 1896, at Loseley Park, Surrey, England, the son of William and Annie Rogers DuPont. He was a great-grandson of E.I. DuPont de Nemours, founder of the DuPont Co. William was educated at St. Paul's School in Concord, New Hampshire, and St. Luke's School in Wayne, Pennsylvania, where he was active in athletics, including tennis, soccer and marksmanship. During World War I, DuPont was plant manager of the Ball Grain Explosives Co. in Guyencourt, Delaware.

He became president of the Delaware Trust Co. in November 1922, and became the bank's president on March 15, 1928. At that time he was the city's youngest bank president. Every spring he played host to all members of the bank's staff at Fair Hill. He was a former president of the Wilmington Clearinghouse Association. He was also president of Shapdale, Inc., which owns and operates the Delaware Trust Building. With its twenty-two-story Hercules Tower Addition, the building was at the time the tallest in Wilmington. He was elected a director of the DuPont Co. in 1930 and was a member of the board's committee on audit from 1939 to 1954, when he was elected to the finance committee.

Although conservatives had battled horse racing in Delaware for many years, the state's need for money during the Depression outweighed the supposed "ill effects" of gambling. Although conservatives had traditionally fought the establishment of horse racing in the state, in 1933, legislation was passed to create the Delaware Racing Commission. The state decided to move forward with the legalization of racing as the Great Depression took its toll on the state's finances. In 1935 the state was given the power to grant licenses for the selling of pools by parimutuel machines and to receive wagers "within the enclosure of any horse race meeting licensed and conducted under this act."

William DuPont had grown up surrounded by horses all of his life. His father owned a stable of trotting horses, and his sister owned a horse named Battleship that proved to be successful in its own right. William DuPont began to purchase horses from the Fair Play line of horses, from which Man o' War was bred, and that is how he got involved in horse owning and breeding.

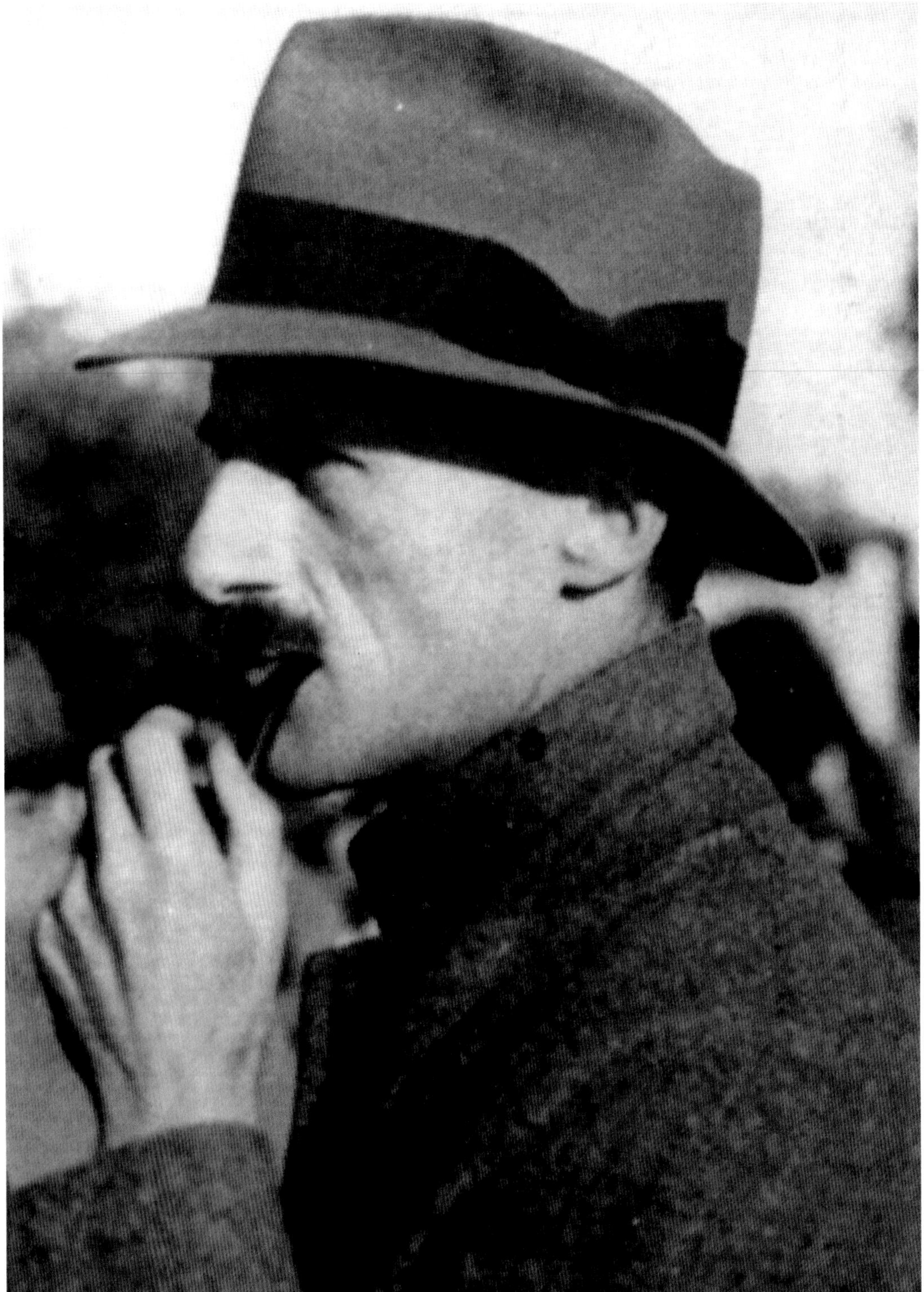

William DuPont at the races. *Reprinted from the* Saturday Evening Post *magazine, © 1957. Saturday Evening Post Society.*

But DuPont had a problem. He owned the large stable at Foxcatcher Farm, at what is known as Fair Hill, Maryland, but just riding the horses for pleasure didn't offer the excitement that he craved. He wanted to put his horses to a real test and challenge. He decided that to achieve his goals, he would have to get involved in horse racing. There were no actual racetracks in Delaware, so he decided that he ought to build one for himself.

In 1936, the Delaware Racing Commission met with the Delaware Steeplechase and Race Association, Inc., a group of five area businessmen including William DuPont Jr. The association submitted a proposal to the commission that was intended to "promote the breeding of thoroughbred horses and the establishment of a race track." The proposal was accepted, and the Delaware Steeplechase and Race Association began to look for a suitable location for the construction of such a track.

DuPont set out one day to scour the countryside to find a suitable location for a track. He got to a place just outside the village of Stanton, Delaware, and looked across the fertile cornfields making up a couple of farms, bisected by the Baltimore and Ohio Railroad. He thought that if he could convince the farmers to sell the land to him it would be an acceptable location. On a second visit to the area, DuPont was at first unable to find the same farms. It was on his third trip to the area that he relocated the farms and purchased them for his racetrack. He bought a total of seven hundred acres at that time.[15]

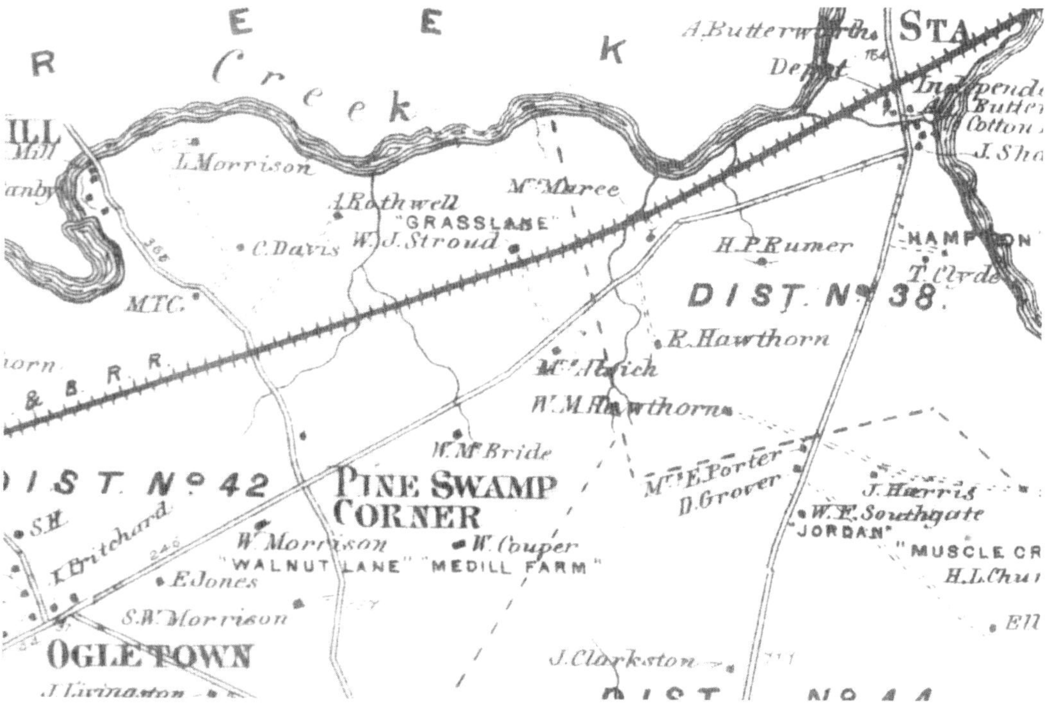

1868 map of the farms to be used for Delaware Park.

Willie DuPont was lean and wiry, often smoking a pipe and wearing a slouchy hat when outdoors. He was described as a man who loved the soil, the countryside and the people who are part of the earth. Friends said there was no music sweeter to his ears than the pound of horses' hooves on the turf. In addition to his contributions at Delaware Park, he was also a member of the executive committee of the Delaware Steeplechase and Race Association and was the author of the state's racing bill. He advocated a policy of high-level racing for the benefit of the public, breeders and owners of horses, and insisted that the sport come before profits for track owners.

As an architect of more than twenty-five horse racing courses, he was recognized internationally as an authority on the design and construction of both steeplechasing and flat-racing tracks. In addition to Delaware Park, he also designed the National Cup Course at Fair Hill, Maryland, a course equivalent to England's Grand National at Aintree. He was called in as a consultant when courses at Belmont Park and Saratoga required reconstruction, and he supervised reconstruction work at Pimlico. DuPont was also the author of a brochure, "How to Build a Track—Plans for a Flat Track."

The DuPonts enriched the turf with flat and steeplechase champions or Hall of Fame members Battleship, Benguala, Berlo, Devil's Bag, Fairy Chant, Go for Wand, Kelso, Mongo, Open Fire, Parlo, Royal Governor, Shipboard, Soothsayer, Tempted and the Mast. Since the 1920s, the DuPont dynasty has spawned such prominent racing stables as Foxcatcher, Montpelier, Bohemia, Christiana, Mooring, Hickory Tree, Brandywine, Roslyn and Hextonia, as well as family members racing under their own names, such as Bayard Sharp, James A. Bayard and Essie DuPont Weir.

William DuPont Jr. acquired eleven thousand acres of Fair Hill's farmland in 1927 so that he could enjoy fox chasing, one of his favorite outdoor activities. He instituted the Fair Hill Steeplechase on the two Saturdays following Labor Day as a benefit for Union Hospital in Elkton, Maryland. He bred and raised horses at another farm, known as Walnut Hall, at Boyce, Virginia. In 1934, as president of the American Foxhound Club, he established the Virginia Hound Show. The Virginia show ran for eight years until it was closed down by the war. It was revived in 1955 and has continued at various locations until the present.

Fair Hill was given over chiefly to Santa Gertrudis cattle, but in every fence at Fair Hill there is a revolving door for horses. This innovation was one of DuPont's designs because he hated to have to dismount to open the various gates. These doors were large, four-sided turnstiles with a steel spindle set in concrete. The rider only had to ride up into one of the pie wedges and grasp a handle to open the gate around the circle to pass through.

DuPont's horses, racing under the silks of Foxcatcher Farms—the name of his stable—won at tracks throughout the nation. He had the distinction of having nominated horses for the Kentucky Derby for a longer period than any other person. Five Foxcatcher horses started in the Derby. One, Dauber, finished second, while another, Hampden, came in third.

At his six-hundred-acre Bellevue estate, north of Wilmington and now made up largely of residential developments, Mr. DuPont maintained a 1¼-mile-long dirt training track with a turf course, steeplechase course and hurdle course in the center

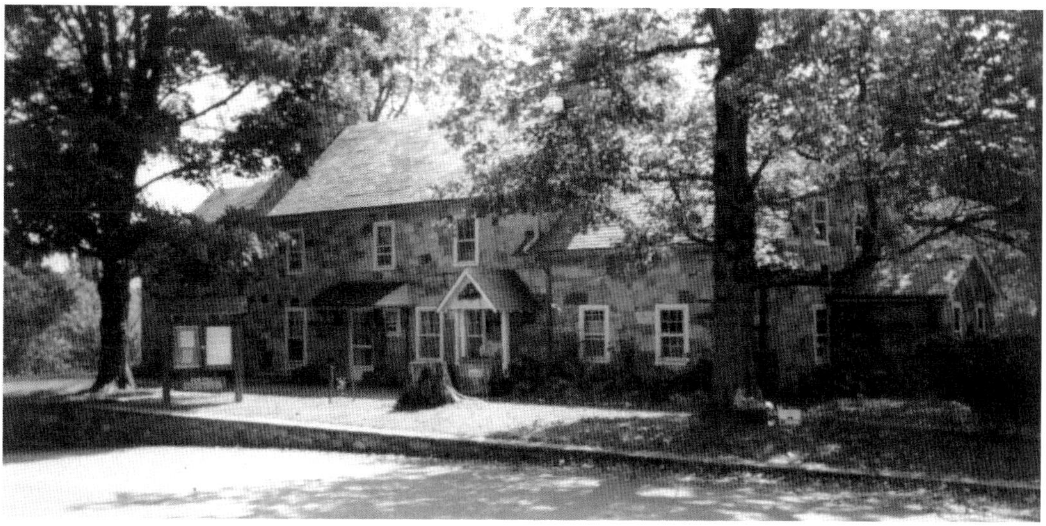

William DuPont's hunting lodge at Fair Hill, now a visitors' center.

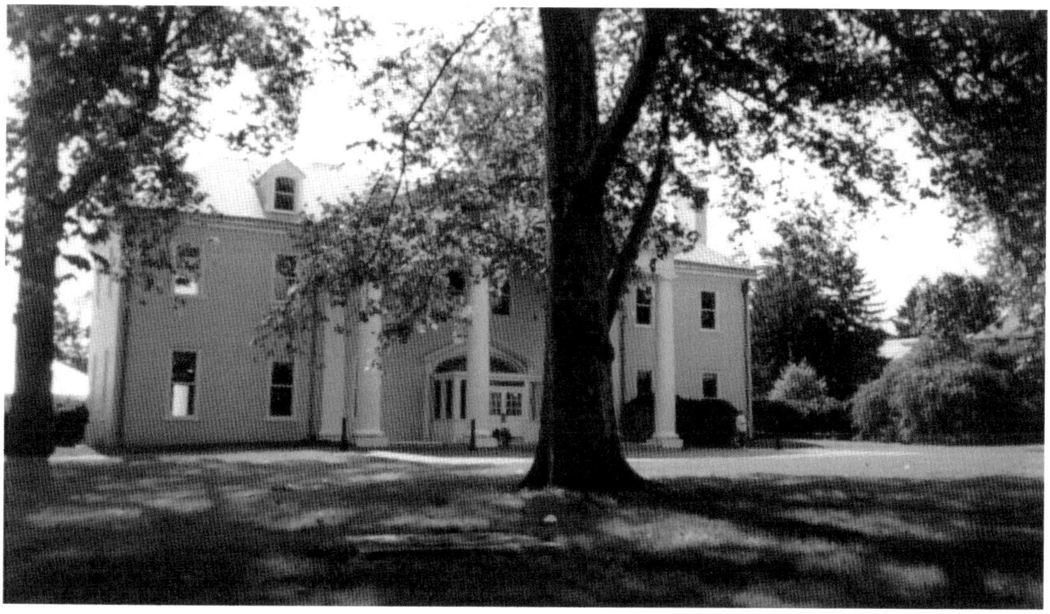

Wiliam DuPont's estate, Belmont, in Wilmington.

of it, and an oval arcade roofed and walls for three-eighths of a mile for inside work. There was also a "figure-eight barn the like of which no man should expect to see twice. It is a monstrous frame building with an earth floor, so huge that a horse can be put up to top speed along the long stroke of the 8." To add to the bucolic nature of the grounds, camellias bloomed and songbirds, squirrels, Australian hares, foxes and wild geese wandered the grounds.

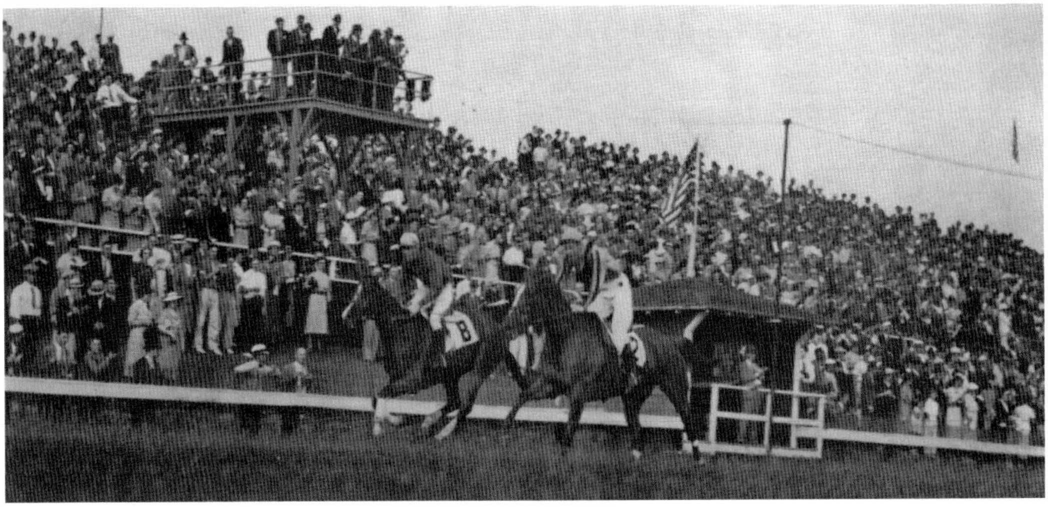

The Foxcatcher National at Fair Hill, Maryland, 1949. *From* Steeplechasing, *Thayer, 1949.*

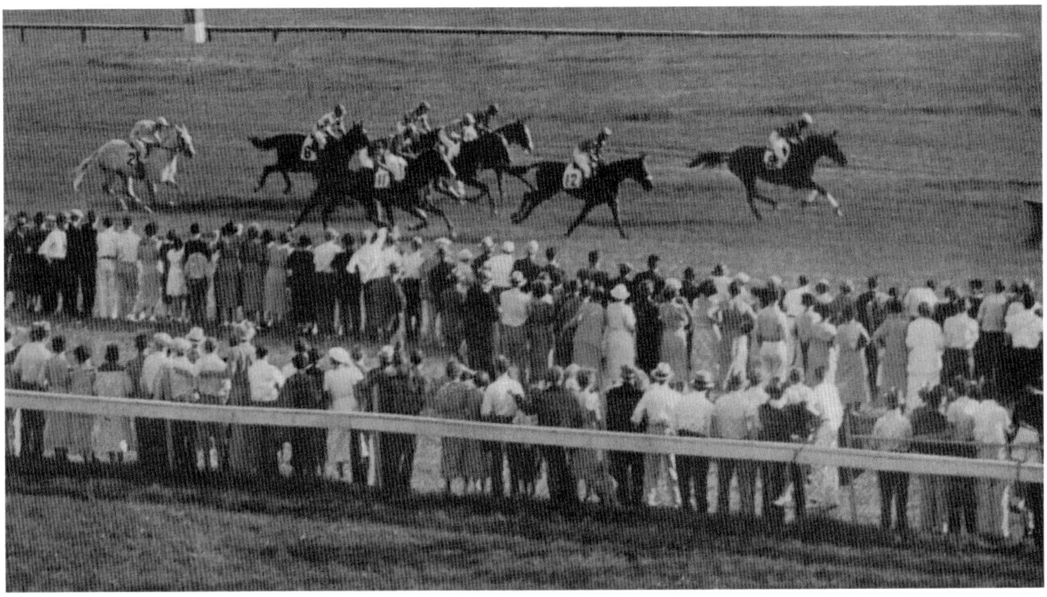

At the finish line of the steeplechase, Foxcatcher National, 1949. *From* Steeplechasing, *Thayer, 1949.*

His experiments and the research he sponsored helped to advance the science of animal husbandry. He helped to further the causes of animal nutrition and the control of animal diseases, including the breeding diseases of horses, equine arthritis, bovine brucellosis, parasite control and distemper. In 1950, the New York Turf Writers Association awarded Mr. DuPont a special plaque for his services in racing.

Second only to his love for horses was his devotion to tennis. Over the years he contributed half the cost of construction of more than sixty all-weather tennis courts in Delaware. Many of them were in special school districts and on the campus of the University of Delaware. In addition he donated money for the construction of public courts in the city.

Mr. DuPont married Miss Jean Liseter Austin on January 1, 1919, in Rosemont, Pennsylvania, and they had four children: Jean Ellen DuPont McConnell Shehan, Evelyn DuPont Donaldson, William Henry DuPont and John Eleuthers DuPont. Mr. and Mrs. DuPont were divorced in February 1941.

DuPont was married for the second time to Margaret Osborne of San Francisco on November 26, 1947, the marriage being performed in a public building by the former Wilmington Mayor Joseph S. Wilson. They had one child, William DuPont III. They were also eventually divorced, on March 27, 1964.[16]

His second wife, Margaret Osborne DuPont, was one of the world's leading tennis players at the time. Margaret DuPont was admired for her incomparable sportsmanship as well as for her unforgettable volleys; she ranked among the top Grand Slam champions, with thirty-seven titles. Beginning in 1942, DuPont joined forces with Louise Brough to form "the greatest of the great" in doubles pairings. The two friends also treated fans to the longest women's singles match in the history of the U.S. championship, a 4–6, 6–4, 15–13 marathon in 1948 that was finally won by DuPont. Among her notable accomplishments were her Grand Slam titles; U.S. Singles Champion 1948–50; U.S. Doubles Champion 1941–50, 1955–57; U.S. Mixed Doubles Champion 1943–46, 1950, 1956, 1958–60; U.S. Hard Court Doubles Champion 1948; Wimbledon Singles Champion 1947; Wimbledon Doubles Champion 1946, 1948–50, 1954; Wimbledon Mixed Doubles Champion 1962; French Singles Champion 1946, 1949; French Doubles Champion 1946–47, 1949; U.S. Wightman Cup Team member 1946–50, 1954–55, 1961–62 (19–0 record), team captain 1953–55, 1957–58, 1961–63, 1965; chair, U.S. Tennis Association (USTA) Wightman Cup Committee, 1954–66; winner of USTA Service Bowl, 1945; inducted into the International Tennis Hall of Fame, 1967; winner of the USTA Educational Merit

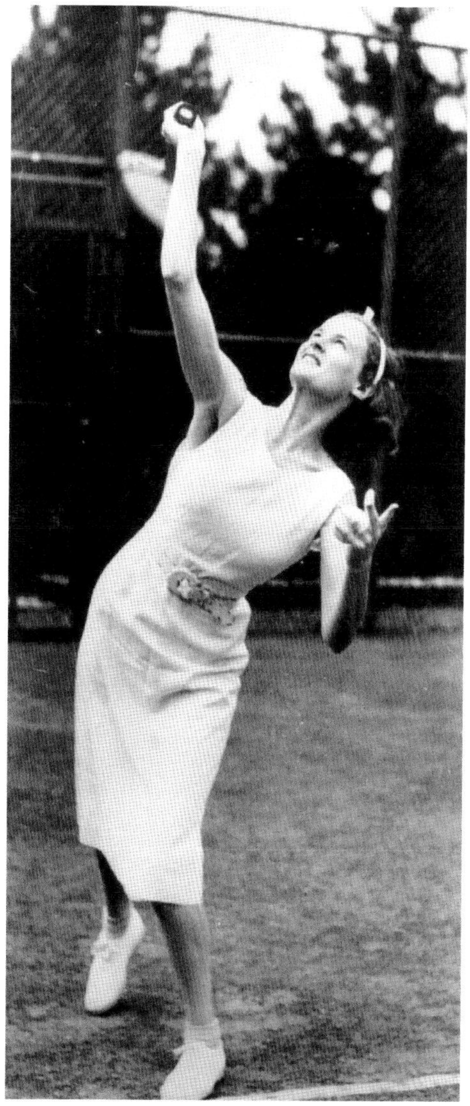

Margaret Osborne DuPont.

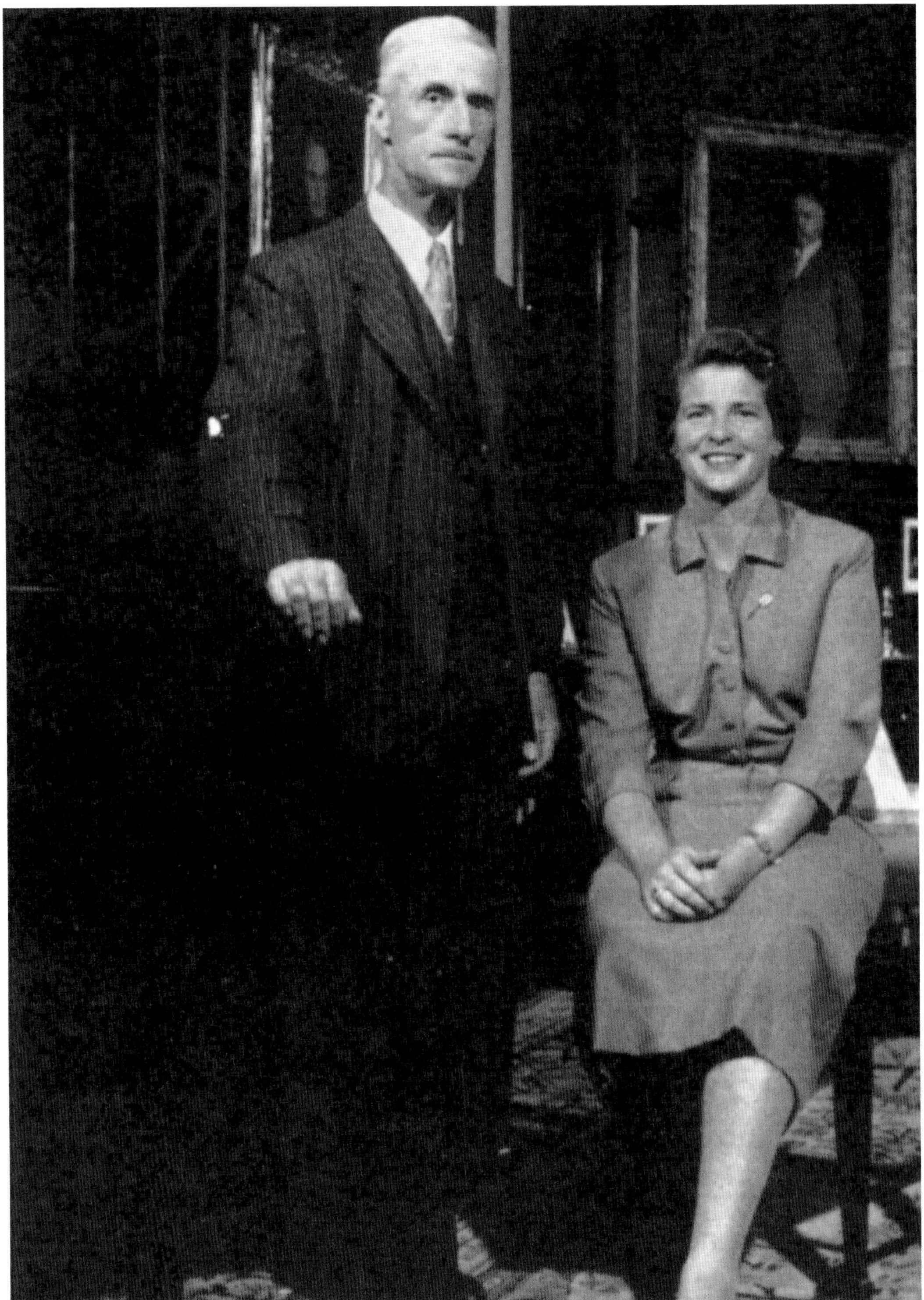

William and Margaret Osborne DuPont. *Reprinted from the* Saturday Evening Post *magazine, © 1957. Saturday Evening Post Society.*

Award, 1974. She was also ranked as a Top 20 Thoroughbred Racehorse Owner by *Thoroughbred Times*, 1996.

At Bellevue, William DuPont supported his wife by building numerous tennis courts: grass, clay, concrete, *en tout cas* and two courts indoors. For her longtime contributions to the game of tennis as a volunteer, coach, teacher and writer, Margaret DuPont was honored with both the USTA's Service Bowl and the Educational Merit Award. Mr. and Mrs. DuPont received the 1957 layman honor awards of the Delaware Association for Health, Physical Education and Recreation for their part in contributing to the growth and interest of tennis in Delaware. He was a past president of the Delaware State Lawn Tennis Association and was given the Community Service Award of Recreation Promotion and Service in 1958. In 1966, after her divorce, Mrs. DuPont moved to El Paso, Texas, where she attended college and joined former doubles partner, Margaret Varner Bloss, in a highly successful second career raising thoroughbred race horses. In 1996, she was elected into the Hall of Fame of the International Tennis Federation.[17]

In 1958, Mr. DuPont gave the City of Wilmington 108 acres, including fifteen tennis courts and a golf course that had formerly been used by the Wilmington Country Club, which was building a new course for use when the lease with Mr. DuPont expired in 1961. The following year he donated 15 adjacent acres to assure the city a full eighteen-hole public course when it officially took possession of the land in 1961. The course was subsequently named Green Hill Golf Course. The land gift, generally considered to be worth upward of $1 million, was described by M. DuPont Lee, then president of the Wilmington Park Commission, as "one of the greatest benefactions done for this city in my lifetime."

Mr. DuPont died at 7:45 p.m. on December 31, 1965, in the Memorial Division of the Delaware Hospital, where he was admitted November 30 and underwent surgery December 9. Hospital officials had listed his condition as poor since the operation.[18] Following the death, most of his extensive landholdings have since been placed into the public trust, and continue to provide a variety of recreational, educational and environmental opportunities for the region. DuPont's home, Bellevue, is maintained by the Delaware Division of Parks and Recreation. Bellevue Hall mansion commands a grand view of this historic estate, and its present form reflects alterations made by William H. DuPont Jr. Mr. DuPont surrounded his home with the finest facilities, including tennis courts, equestrian stables, gardens and a picturesque pond amid woodlands and fields overlooking the Delaware River. Originally acquired by the State of Delaware in 1976, the park now covers 328 acres.

His Fair Hill Farm in Cecil County was donated to the State of Maryland and became home to the annual Fair Hill Games, a celebration of Scottish culture. The hunting lodge was converted into a nature center. An important equestrian healthcare and training facility was added. Soon, an adjacent property will also hold a world-class golf course, replacing the aging Newark Country Club in Delaware.

The estate that he held in Bozman, Talbot County, Reinecke Fuchs Farm, has morphed into something he might never have imagined. But considering his deep love for the outdoors and nature, it seems certain he would be pleased with what it has become: the Jean Ellen DuPont Shehan Audubon Center and Sanctuary. DuPont's daughter, Mrs. Jean DuPont Shehan, donated the entire 952 acres of private forest, field, marsh and jagged coastline on Chesapeake Bay's Eastern Shore to the Audubon Society, on the promise that the land would be converted to a public nature center and sanctuary. Jean DuPont Shehan had been raised at Liseter Hall in Philadelphia, but grew up at Foxcatcher Farm, learning to ride horses both in the English and sidesaddle styles. She was fond of both the carriage shows and the hunting field there, and adopted her father's passion for the nature and excitement of Foxcatcher Farm.[19] So the legacy of Willie DuPont lives on, not only in the lives of his own children, but also in the countless others who benefited from his life and loves.

William DuPont's sister, Marion DuPont Scott, also made notable contributions to the horse racing industry. She lived at the family estate of Montpelier, Orange County, Virginia, and had a residence at Holly Hedge in Camden, South Carolina, where she developed the Camden Training Center for stabling and training thoroughbred horses. From her youth she was interested in the breeding and raising of fine horses, first hunting horses and later thoroughbreds. In 1934, Mrs. Scott and her brother William established the Montpelier Races. For many years she was the hostess of these races, of which she was also the honorary chairwoman.

One of Mrs. Scott's most famous horses was Battleship, sired by the great Man o' War. After winning the Grand National Steeplechase Handicap at Belmont Park in 1934, and other notable races in America, Battleship became the first American-bred and American-owned horse to win the Grand National Steeplechase at Aintree, England, in 1938. Subsequently, Battleship retired to stud at Montpelier and, along with Annapolis, another son of Man o' War that was owned by Mrs. Scott, sired many outstanding horses. She was also the owner of Mongo, a son of Royal Charger and Accra. Among other races, Mongo won the Washington, D.C. International at Laurel, Maryland, and the United Nations Handicap at Atlantic City, New Jersey, for two successive years. In 1963, he was declared the Champion Grass Horse of America, and after winning purses aggregating in excess of $800,000 was retired to stud at Blue Ridge Farm near Upperville, Virginia, where he stood as a successful sire until his death in early 1983.[20]

The Construction of Delaware Park

Horses lend us the wings we lack.
—author unknown

In the history of the country, 1937 was a relatively quiet, hopeful year. President Roosevelt was leading the country out of the Depression with his New Deal; rain was beginning to fall in the Western United States, ending years of drought that had caused the Dust Bowl; and the Nazis had yet to show their true colors. It was a time when Americans began to enjoy life again, to look to the future with a shared optimism that hadn't been felt since 1928.

In March, the first issue of *Detective Comics* was published, and in its issue #27 Batman was born to the world. On March 27, the Golden Gate Bridge opened for traffic in San Francisco. Edgar Bergen and Glenn Miller made their debuts. Walt Disney Studios released its first full-length classic, *Snow White and the Seven Dwarfs*. The epic novel *Gone with the Wind* was given the Pulitzer Prize for fiction. On June 22, Joe Lewis defeated James J. Braddock in the eighth round at a fight in the middle of Comisky Park in Chicago.

The year 1937 was not without its troublesome points. Nazi Germany was beginning to rise, and Stalin began his biggest attempt to date to eliminate dissidents and establish his own brand of Communism. On May 6, the Hindenburg burst into flames at Lakehurst, New Jersey, and the world listened to the horror on the radio as the event was broadcast live. A civil war raged in Spain, and some of the attacks were linked to German airplanes. On May 27, seventy thousand steel workers went on strike, seriously threatening Roosevelt's economic recovery plans. The strike lasted for months and eventually resulted in the National Guard being called out to quell violence in Johnstown, Pennsylvania, and elsewhere. On July 2, Amelia Earhart disappeared over Howland Island in her attempt to be the first woman to fly around the globe.

Locally, construction throughout the area began to rise for the first time in seven years. Braunstein's Clothing Store in Wilmington had dresses for $8.00 and raincoats for $3.00; Miller's was selling Simmons mattresses for $17.95; Sears, Roebuck and Co.

had bedroom suites for $68.80 and Kenmore vacuums for $22.45; and Eckerd's Drugs had Dr. West Toothpaste, Cocomelt and Noxzema. The Delaware Motor Car Co. was selling La Salle V-8s, Hudsons and Studebakers. The main news source was the *Journal Every Evening*, precursor to the *Wilmington News-Journal*, and its comic section thrilled children with the episodes of "Alley Oop," "Freckles and His Friends Toots and Casper" and "Myra North, Special Nurse." The Wilmington Police Department was adding two-way radios to its cars, a new invention for crime fighting. And at the Lowe's Theater in Wilmington, patrons were presented with the premiere of two summertime films destined to become classics: *A Day at the Races*, starring the Marx brothers, and *Captains Courageous*, with Lionel Barrymore and Spencer Tracy.

Near the proposed site of Delaware Park, things were much quieter. Long before the area had been developed into a complex of housing developments and shopping centers, in 1937 this was still farmland, dirt roads and scattered villages like Stanton and Christiana. Even the college town of Newark was still largely undeveloped, with only Main Street and Delaware Avenue having shops and college facilities.

William DuPont hired Edward Burke to oversee the development of the racetrack. Burke was then the general manager of the racetrack at Havre de Grace, Maryland. He had been associated with horse racing since 1885 as a fan, handicapper and builder of the racetracks at Jamaica, New York, and Havre de Grace. DuPont threatened Burke into the job in a way, promising to bankrupt his operation at Havre de Grace with "murderous competition." Within twenty-four hours of the offer, Burke sent DuPont a telegram in which he accepted the job.[21] The news of his appointment to the position of general manager was made on January 28, 1937.[22] In addition to Burke, DuPont also encouraged other horse racing professionals from Havre de Grace and Pimlico to quit their jobs to come work for him.

Burke's dazzling shock of white hair and flowing white mustache made him a remarkable figure at racetracks, but at Havre de Grace he customarily sat out most programs in the mutual plant. He commented that he did so "to avoid being a sucker. Anybody with any kind of sob story can get money out of me. If I stayed in the office I'd be broke. They can't find me so easily here."[23]

Construction of the facility in Stanton began in the summer of 1936. The racetrack was well serviced by both the Baltimore and Ohio Railroad and the Pennsylvania Railroad, which operated adjacent lines that could be used to stop at this location and ferry passengers directly into a short walk to the grandstand. DuPont also had built spacious parking lots for cars, as well as a reserved lot next to the grandstand for the owners, jockeys and other staff holding a parking pass. As originally built, an underground tunnel ran from the grandstand to the public parking lot on the opposite side of the train lines. The original stands and grandstand had a capacity of 7,500 people.

In addition to the flat track, there were two steeplechase courses with fourteen jumps located in the infield, one slightly under a mile and the other a two-mile jaunt. The longer course crossed over the main flat track at the head of the back stretch, went off at an angle and came back again to cross the flat track. The finish was directly in front of the grandstand.

There was no steeplechase racing at Delaware Park that first year, because of the need to develop an adequate sod. It was thought that in time the steeplechase courses at Delaware Park would be superior to any in the country, excelling even the strips at Belmont and the Aqueduct. The soil at Delaware Park, with its heavy clay base, is natural grass land, while the Long Island soil, sandy and porous with a gravel base, is not the proper type for racing sod. Rain water filters through it as fast as it falls. Because of this, the keepers at the Aqueduct had to continuously add top dressing to the steeplechase course.[24]

The stables, comprising stalls for more than 1,500 horses and housing some of the finest thoroughbreds in the country, were situated about a quarter-mile from the home turn. They were ultramodern, with living quarters at the end of each for the grooms. The stables were separated at least one hundred feet apart as a firefighting precaution. The stable area was enclosed in an eighteen-foot fence of the heaviest wire mesh and it was electrically charged at night to forestall "night riders" and "spongers." (Night riders are thieves who would make off with the horses under cover of night. Spongers are those who would place sponges or fabric inside a horse's nose to cause it to slow during a race.) On opening day, guards were placed at the entrance to the stables to bar anyone without the proper identification from entering the area and potentially injuring or otherwise affecting the horses there.

The administration building near the paddock and saddling ring was a two-story frame structure with six rooms on the first floor and a large room and bathing facilities on the second. The jockeys' weighing-in room, office of the racing secretary, steward's room, general office space and horsemen's lobby were all situated in the first floor of the building. Large rooms in the second floor were used as the jockeys' waiting rooms. The first and second floors were equipped with porches, with the second-floor porch facing the track.

The saddling ring between the paddock and the clubhouse side of the grandstand was flawless and was one of the finest found wherever the horses pound the turf. Rare shrubbery and beautiful shade trees dotted the carpet-like sod in the wire-fenced enclosure where the horses were saddled.

In addition to the grandstand, administration and paddock, numerous other modern structures covered the huge plant. The medical and saliva test building was located on the north lawn, while the bunkhouses and cook house were situated in various sections of the stable area.

Three parking areas accommodated more than five thousand automobiles. The general parking area inside the main gateway on the Wilmington-Newark Road (now Kirkwood Highway) cared for about three thousand vehicles, while the club parking area between the flat track and the lawn plaza and spurs of the sidings of the Pennsylvania Railroad, and the section on the other side of the sidings between the Baltimore and Ohio main line to the northwest of the track proper, each held more than one thousand automobiles.

Like other racing plants in the country, Delaware Park had direct-to-the-track service for its race devotees. Both the Pennsylvania Railroad and the Baltimore and Ohio Railroad had swung spurs into the park leading up to loading and unloading platforms within a few strides of the ticket windows and track entrances. More than two miles of railroad siding accommodating more than fifty railroad cars had been laid within the grounds. Another siding swung off the Pennsylvania Railroad spur just as it entered the plant in the rear of the stables for the loading and unloading of horses and material that may be taken to and from the track.

Construction of the huge racing plant was under the direction of Bernard T. Converse, engineer for the Delaware Steeplechase and Race Association, and under the general supervision of William DuPont Jr. and the other directors of the association. The supervisor of construction was Frank M. Kelly of Texas, who had directed the construction of some of the finest racecourses in America.[25]

Wark and Company of Philadelphia, the general contractor for the plant, erected the grandstand, stables, administration building and other buildings, and sublet considerable work throughout the large layout to more than a dozen subcontractors. The work was started in June of 1936 and kept more than 100 workmen busy for a year. Their advertisement in a special opening day section of the *Wilmington Morning News* boasted, "300 men employed to erect 3 million feet of lumber used in construction of the Grand Stand, Administration Buildings, and 75 additional buildings, comprised of stables, bunk houses, feed barns, kitchens, etc. Completed in Five (5) Months."

George & Lynch, Wilmington and Dover road builders and excavation contractors, installed the water lines, did the grading for the steeplechase and flat track and installed the drainage for the facility. The company also put down the Amiesite (asphalt) drives. Included in the work was the laying of about forty-five hundred feet of water lines through the grounds for supplying water for the track, the grandstand, stables and paddock. Water was obtained through the Delaware Water Company owned by the Pennsylvania Railroad, which had assured the association a water supply up to one million gallons a day if necessary.

John A. Bader II, a Wilmington contractor and builder who had just completed the indoor training track for Donald P. Ross adjacent to Delaware Park, erected the tall, white lattice gates and other attractive gateways throughout the spacious course. Savery & Cooke of Wilmington, ornamental and miscellaneous ironworkers, completed all the ornamental ironwork throughout the grandstand and other sections of the facility, including all the ornamental iron railings.

The N.B. Mancill Construction Company of Wilmington, which had previously constructed the track for William DuPont at Bellevue, did considerable grading and graveling throughout the layout. The company made the excavation for the Pennsylvania Railroad spur into Delaware Park; graded and graveled the parking fields, stables and grandstand; and put in the fill for the gallery.

Several bungalows built by the Van Sant Brothers, a local building and contracting firm, were modern in every detail and added considerably to the ultramodern trend throughout the facility.

The electrical work in the parimutuel machines, the radio amplification systems and the photoelectric cells for the finish of a race were installed by the Robinson Electric Company of Philadelphia, which also completed the wiring in the grandstand clubhouse, stables and service buildings. The McHugh Electric Company of Wilmington installed transformers and all in-line wiring in the plant.

Structural steel work on the huge grandstand was furnished and erected by the Belmont Iron Works of Philadelphia. The Otis Elevator Company, also of Philadelphia, installed the elevator service to the club level of the grandstand. The plumbing work in the restrooms, the fountains, the shower houses, the hot water houses in the stables and other plumbing throughout the facility was completed by W. Anderson and Company of Philadelphia.

Some fourteen thousand arborvitae plants, sycamores, maples and other herbaceous trees were set out about the entrance, the track, the saddling ring, the grandstand and other sections of the park by William H. Dovie Inc. of Berwyn, Pennsylvania. The painting of the grandstand was done by Juennie Barker Company and the stables, administration and other buildings by Henry S, Rau, both Philadelphia concerns.

It was the ground itself that offered the biggest challenge during the construction of the park. The farms that DuPont purchased were within the floodplain of the Christiana Creek, a water course that flooded frequently. This silty soil was well suited to farming, but when it rained the entire course turned into slimy mud. DuPont turned to Clarke Pardee, a former naval officer who had been hired as track superintendent, who sat for days and days making mud pies in the middle of the track, trying to find a solution to the muddy problems. "You pack the earth into a cake and soak it with water," he explained. "Then you bake it. That's what happens when the sun dries out a wet track. Now you tap it"—he rapped his desk with a gold pencil—"and if it pops open, that's how the clods will crumble under horses' feet." Pardee eventually resolved that issue by bringing in fill materials with more clay in them and adding drainage piping throughout the track where necessary.

The new park attracted some of the most notable horses in the area. "Among the horses listed to race at Delaware were the Foxcatcher Farms of William DuPont, Mr. and Mrs. Walter M. Jeffords, J.P. Jones, Mrs. Louise Viau, Alfred Vanderbilt, Glen Riddle Farm, including War Admiral, one of the greatest three-year-olds of all times; E.K. Bryson, E.R. Bradley and any number of owners of smaller strings."[26]

William DuPont maintained an endless energy with all of his pursuits. His love for all of the hunting sports was his lifetime passion, and Delaware Park was his greatest success and crowning achievement. Even in his later years, long after the park had proven itself, he was characterized as a man of youthful excitement about everything he chose to devote his attention to. "At sixty-one, the laird of the manor can take a wiry young companion out at dawn behind the hounds, chase foxes, shoot quail, geese and ducks all day, and stride springily home at nightfall, to arise again at four while his guests are laid out like cordwood. This is the man who, with nothing else to do, built Delaware Park."[27]

But the park, and the return of horse racing and its concurrent gambling, was not without controversy by the moralists who still worried about the degradation of values that would result. An editorial appeared in the *Newark Post* on June 24, 1937, just a few days before the grand opening, in which it was stated,

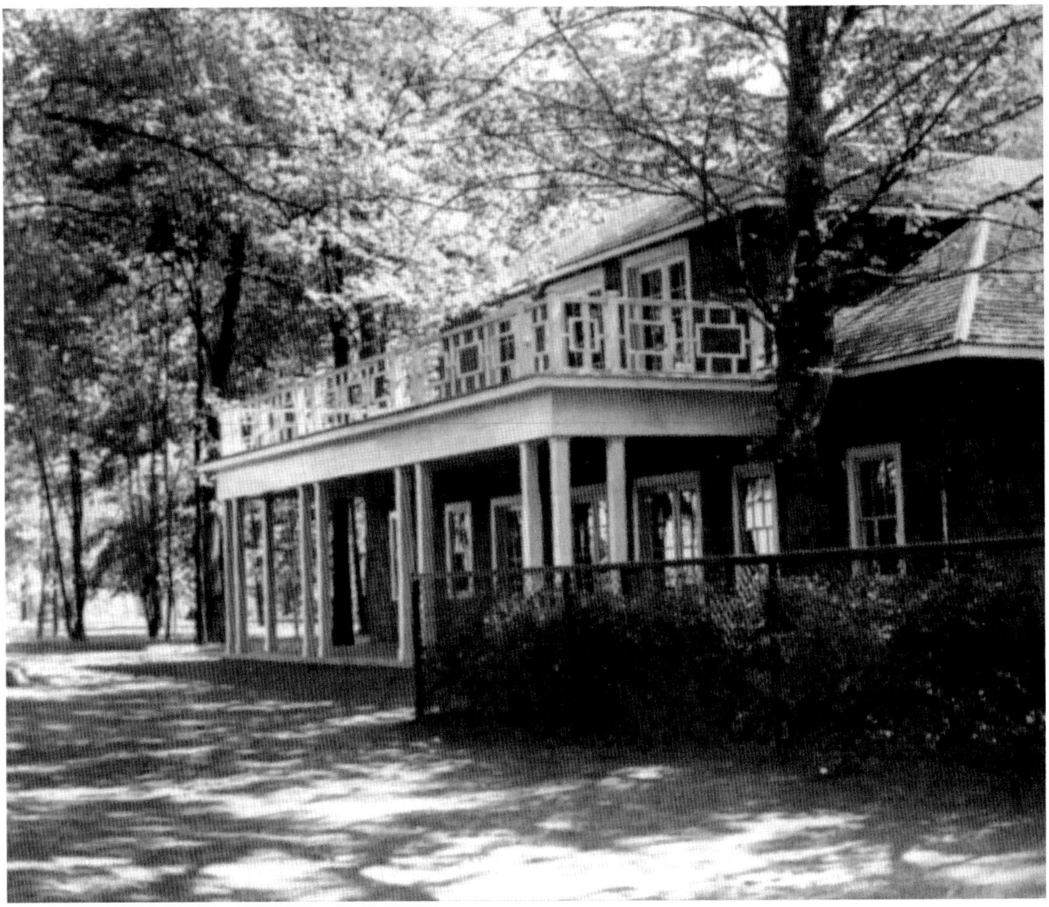

Administration building behind the paddock. *Reprinted from the* Saturday Evening Post *magazine, © 1957. Saturday Evening Post Society.*

> [The] *inauguration of horse racing and legalized gambling this week can, in a financial sense, do a lot of good—or bad—for the community in general. It depends entirely upon how the community handles racing and its manifold temptations to reap something for nothing…That it is impossible to "beat" the horses is a certainty. Regarded as a sport and when taken in small doses, racing can provide many pleasant afternoons for the average individual. Any and all attempts to take the ponies to the cleaners, so to speak, however, will prove more than costly, especially for the unsuspecting novice, who thought beginners luck or blind chance might happen to have a few shekels riding on a long shot's break. Some Delaware people, who have never seen anything but a plow horse before, will strike that kind of luck at the outset. These same people will be wise to remember the axiom about the good beginning bringing a sad ending.*[28]

Originally there were plans underway to have the great horse War Admiral, son of Man o' War, at opening day at the park. His participation was dependant upon how he would run several weeks before at the Belmont Stakes, but it was being touted as a great opportunity for Delawareans to see one of the best-known names in thoroughbred racing at the time.[29] However, War Admiral stumbled coming out of the gate at Belmont on June 6, and Glen Riddle Farm owner Samuel Riddle and his trainer, George Conway, decided to keep War Admiral at his home stable at Saratoga for a few weeks to rest.[30]

Another well-known horse that had originally been slated to appear on opening day was Rosemont, who had recently won at San Antonio and Santa Anita, winning purses totaling $97,000. Owned by William DuPont Jr., Rosemont was scheduled to run in the Brandywine, Sussex and New Castle Handicaps.[31] Later it was announced that Aneroid, hero of the fastest Suburban Handicap ever run, was also promised to appear. Owned by J.A. Manfuso of Washington, Aneroid was the son of the steed Porter.[32]

On May 27, disaster was narrowly averted when a freak storm arose and a small tornado passed just outside of the boundaries of the racetrack. State Senator Donald P. Ross was constructing an indoor training track for his horses on a parcel of land immediately adjacent to the racetrack, and the funnel cloud destroyed eight hundred feet of the track. Thankfully, neither the barns nor the nearly completed grandstands at Delaware Park was damaged by this storm.[33]

Amid the flurry of activity to complete the racetrack for its scheduled opening, William DuPont and his family were already having success on a different track. At the Devon Horse Show held on May 28, 1937, Miss Jean DuPont, fourteen-year-old daughter of William DuPont, rode her old horse Seaside to victory in the children's jumping competition. The jumps were placed at three feet, six inches. Later, the entire family won blue ribbons in the family saddle class as well.[34]

On June 3, James P. Ross, track superintendent, announced that although work would still be ongoing to complete the grandstand and put finishing touches elsewhere, the stables and track would be ready by June 12 for anyone who wanted to bring their horses early to train. Ross said, "As a matter of fact, none of the owners have asked for the use of the track for training purposes yet. No one wants to come this early."[35] Charles Baker Jr. added that the work was progressing rapidly and he fully expected the track, grounds and equipment to be ready for opening day.

The last hurdle to the park was jumped on June 10, 1937, when during a meeting of the Jockey Club, it "granted approval to the Delaware Steeplechase and Racing Association to conduct racing at Delaware Park in Stanton, Delaware. The dates were June 26 to July 24, inclusive."[36] While the park was still under construction, an article in the *New York Times* appeared, giving the new park nothing but praise. It reported that this park was "in a natural setting of trees and rolling hills…one of the most beautiful in America."[37]

The anticipated crowds began to cause a major concern to the New Castle County government. Since this part of the county was still underdeveloped, no one had given much though to the infrastructure needed to safely bring thousands of cars to the racetrack. Many of the roads in its vicinity were still gravel, and there were only a few intersections marked with any kind of stop signs or other directional signage. Adding to the concern was the Old Capital Trail, between Prices Corner and Marshallton. This narrow, winding road became a single lane when it passed under the Baltimore and Ohio Railroad Bridge. Turning lanes were added on Capital Trail to permit the long lines of cars to have safe access into the park. The state police and the Department of Transportation began to envision a traffic nightmare on opening day as thousands of excited horse racing fans attempted to travel to the rural countryside.[38]

Another concern that was raised before opening day was the availability of liquor. Liquor sales were expressly forbidden at the track itself, because of the concern that the combination of gambling and alcohol would have disastrous effects. Just before the track opened, the State Liquor Commission ordered that all liquor sales within a quarter-mile of the track, even at licensed outlets, be banned on race days. There was little that could be done about patrons buying it from more distant sources, but it was hoped that this would reduce the amount of alcoholic consumption at the track.[39]

In response to this alcoholic ban, the Hotel DuPont in Wilmington decided to take its Parlor O and turn it into a Turf Club. The more elite patrons of the sport could buy their entrance tickets there, so as to bypass what were anticipated to be long lines at the track ticket office, and also enjoy their selection of food and beverages in comfort before the races. The hotel staffed the room with the current major newspapers and racing papers for their use as well. Mr. Gregson, hotel manager at the time, said that the Turf Club could also be used for private parties by the members of the club.[40]

At the last moment, Samuel Riddle changed his mind and shipped War Admiral and nine other thoroughbreds to Delaware Park, not to race but at least to be a part of the excitement of opening day.[41] The nine other horses from Glen Riddle Farm arriving that day were Prince Alone, Warrior Queen, Great Blaze, Army Banner, Firing, Rise and Shine, Great Gun, First Alarm and All Afire.

Three special railroad carloads were arranged to bring the horses in from distant parts, and many others arrived in trailers over the surface roadways. The air was filled with dust and hay as the confusing mass of horses, trainers, jockeys and aides led their horses from the train platforms and the parking area to their assigned stables. More than two hundred horses arrived that day, headed by nine belonging to Mrs. C. Oliver Iselin. The Iselin string was headed by Strabo, who had captured the Dwyer Stakes at Belmont the previous week and was one of the nominees for the upcoming Kent Handicap. There were also fifteen horses belonging to W.J. Hirsch, headed by Columbiana, the winner of the recent Widener Handicap. Tranquility Farms shipped in twenty-six horses and arrived with noted jockey Basil James, who was slated to ride Tranquility Farms' entrants at Delaware Park.[42]

Also of note was Flying Scot, the son of the Porter and Caledonia. The colt had been beaten by Reaping Reward and Eagle Pass in the last Latonia Derby, but must have improved considerably to garner the hopes of his owner, Jock Whitney. Flying Scot would be the top weight in the Kent under 122 pounds in the absence of War Admiral, and Eagle Pass, his rival of the Latonia Derby, would pack 121.[43]

As the sun rose on Delaware Park the following day, it was a glorious sight as hundreds of horses began to practice around the track. At the same time, finishing touches were being put on the grandstand and everything was being prepared for the opening day crowd. The totalizer was being tested, and mutuel ticket sellers and cashiers assembled to practice under the supervision of H.M. Frank, who had come here from the Ak-Sar-Ben track at Omaha, Nebraska, to oversee the financial end of the operations. It was expected that the windows would be full on opening day, with 125 sellers and 100 cashiers.[44]

On the eve of the grand opening of Delaware Park, a gala supper was presented in the clubroom of the Hotel DuPont in honor of the officials of the Delaware Steeplechase and Racing Association and the Delaware State Racing Commission. Among the attendees were Earl Sande, three-time winner of the Kentucky Derby; Governor Richard C. McMullen; Wilmington Mayor Walter C. Bacon; President of the City Council Albert W. James; and James R. Morford, city solicitor. Also at the supper were Charles W. Baker, president of the race association, and Donald P. Ross, president of the Delaware Turf Club.[45] At the beginning of the banquet, famous broadcaster Clem McCarthy announced on nationwide radio broadcast that the park was formally open. Clem McCarthy had been thrilling racing fans for years with his gravel-voiced, machine-gun accounts of horse races. McCarthy described every Kentucky Derby from 1928 to 1937, and some after as well. On the night of the banquet, he had just returned from broadcasting the Braddock-Louis fight the week before in Chicago. He commented, "You have a lovely course here, the grandstand is comparable to any in the country, and you have the most beautiful paddock of any track I have seen."[46]

C.W. Baker Jr., president of the Delaware Steeplechase and Race Association, discussed the careful preparations for the twenty-eight-day meeting. He assured the press and public alike that the owners of the better stables in the country were cooperating with the new park and that Delaware would have a successful entry into the horse racing world.[47]

Governor Richard C. McMullen pointed to the favorable location at Delaware and Wilmington for racing. He expected and predicted, "We want everyone to enjoy the races and carry away pleasant recollections to our city and our State. Wilmington will offer the best in racing, but it will be just as difficult to pick the winners here as anywhere else in the country."[48]

Rather than attending the gala at the Hotel DuPont, William DuPont addressed the crowd at the University Club in Wilmington, where he stated that only the best stables in the country would compete at Delaware Park and gave a presentation on the history of thoroughbred racing in America to the guests. He traced the origin of the Arabian horse and the development of the English racing horse and the American race horse. He said that English steeplechasing was the best type at present, but that the steady growth of that phase in this country would soon challenge the English supremacy. He also showed the crowd of 150 visitors four films depicting steeplechasing in England, at Pimlico and at the Kentucky Derby.[49]

Restaurant and hotel men also prepared for the heavy influx of visitors to the city. At the Hotel DuPont, new lunch facilities that were able to care for 250 people were added to the mezzanine floor. Seizing the opportunity for some easy money, a number of local people erected roadside stands selling food and drinks, and businessmen constructed new gas stations on the routes to and from the track, where "new gas stations and lunch counters are numerous."[50]

Closer to the racetrack, all available rooms at boardinghouses in Stanton, Newark and Marshallton were filled with eager fans. Virtually every available hotel room from Newark to Wilmington was full of excited patrons, although some greedy operators began to ask as much as the exorbitant seventeen dollars a night and were left with empty rooms. The local restaurants and taverns teemed with excitement.

The county directed that all buses from Marshallton and Newark were to run directly to the track, at fifteen-minute intervals. Finally, all twenty-two state policemen in New Castle County were posted at key points to direct traffic to the park.[51]

The weekend before opening, longtime *Washington Post* columnist Walter Haight happened to stop by the new park en route from Belmont. He recounted that on a quiet Sunday morning just before the park was to open, he was traveling down Route 40 and decided to turn off and visit the new park for himself. Nobody was around as he walked through the stands, but then he spotted a man "wearing muddied work shoes, khaki pants and an open shirt to match, and an old battered brown felt hat." As he drew closer, he realized the man was William DuPont himself, nailing nails into the seats in the grandstand until the seats were secured to his liking. This was the love and devotion that DuPont had for this track and for the years of excitement that it promised to him and many others like him. The day after DuPont died thirty years later, Haight remembered that chance meeting and commented that "perhaps not as important as the gold spike that completed the transcontinental railroad, but befitting was the last nail he drove that day—the finishing touch on Delaware Park, now a memorial to a good racing man."[52]

Opening Day and Early Events

Any man who likes a cayuse is a friend of mine…I never knew a horse lover who was a mean man.
—author unknown

The new $1 million park had its opening day to much excitement on June 26, 1937, with a thirty-day meet. Crowds began to stream into the area days before the race. Race fans arrived from far and near. An estimated twenty to twenty-five thousand people filled the clubhouse, stands and terrace. The Baltimore and Ohio Railroad, which had constructed a station for the park, operated a special train from Wilmington to Delaware Park for the sum of thirty cents round trip.

The original Delaware Park facilities consisted of an open-air, 7,500-seat grandstand with an innovative tiered clubhouse/turf club on the upper level. The track itself was a one-mile dirt oval with a pair of steeplechase turf courses. The backstretch contained stables for 1,226 horses. The outstanding features of Delaware Park were the exquisite architecture and the saddling and picnic grove areas. The signature track feature is a cedar wood paddock and large walking ring in a hedged park. It can be viewed through the grove area and terraces off each clubhouse level. As described in the news of the day, the track was complete with a racing strip visible from every part of the grandstand, two steeplechase courses modeled after Aintree in England, stalls for 1,500 horses in well-ventilated stables surrounded by a fifteen-foot wire fence and a beautiful paddock modeled after the paddocks at Belmont and Saratoga.[53]

Unlike other racetracks across the country, DuPont decided from the first that he wanted his racecourse to offer enjoyment for the entire family. In New York it was deemed somewhat of a sin to bring children to the track, but DuPont mandated that a lovely playground be built and that children be allowed in for a special rate of twenty cents. No doubt it was his own fond memories of a childhood surrounded by horses that caused him to want to share his track with generations of children. He furthered this cause by banning the sale of liquor at the park, except in the turf club.[54] It actually wasn't until 1965 that beer was offered at the park, with harder liquor offered for the first time in 1966.[55] Delaware Park was also praised in *Time* magazine after its opening, which reported that a

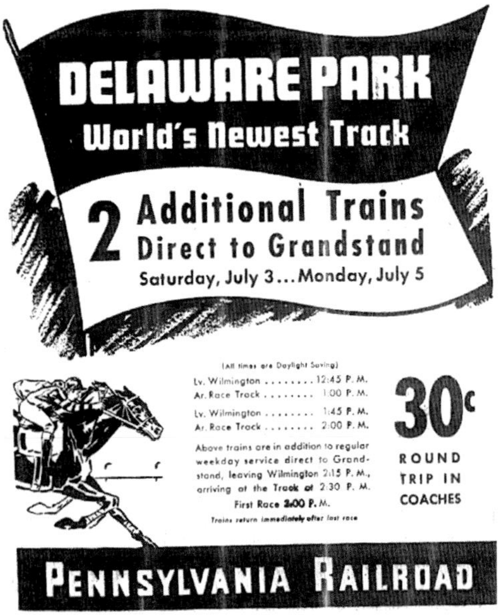

Advertisement for Pennsylvania Railroad, 1937.

"noteworthy feature of the plant is a lawn that slopes sharply down from the grandstand to the track to permit spectators to see races without going back to their seats."[56]

Early on opening day, thousands of cars began to pass through Wilmington, many from other states, converging on Delaware Park. Police reported that drivers were courteous and no accidents were reported. Opening day was a beautiful warm spring day, with blue skies to greet the throng of visitors. Delaware Governor Richard C. McMullen, Secretary of State Charles L. Terry and other state and local dignitaries occupied boxes near the finish line. Pennsylvania Governor George H. Earle arrived by train at 2:30 p.m. Another noted celebrity on hand was Colonel E.R. Bradley, whose Idle Hour Farm colors had been carried to victory at the Kentucky Derby three times. Mrs. William DuPont and State Senator Donald P. Ross were also present.

Surprisingly absent from the opening day festivities was its host, William DuPont Jr. DuPont decided to spend the weekend at the Aqueduct track in New York to watch Rosemont, his handicap star of Foxcatcher Farms, run in the $20,000 Brooklyn Handicap.[57]

Clem McCarthy was still on hand to assist regular radio announcer Cris Wood Jr. in describing the race to a national audience. McCarthy broadcast the Kent Handicap over the National Broadcasting Company at 5:15 p.m.

The excitement of the crowd was furthered by the world-class collection of jockeys who appeared at opening day. There was Charley Kurtsinger of Louisville, Kentucky, who had raced War Admiral to the Triple Crown in 1937 at the Kentucky Derby, Preakness and Belmont Stakes; and Harry Richards, pilot of Fairy Hill in the Santa Anita Derby and of Rosemont in the Santa Anita Handicap in the silks of William DuPont Jr. Also appearing in the race at Delaware that day were Joe Renick, Eddie Arcaro and Raymond "Sonny" Workman.

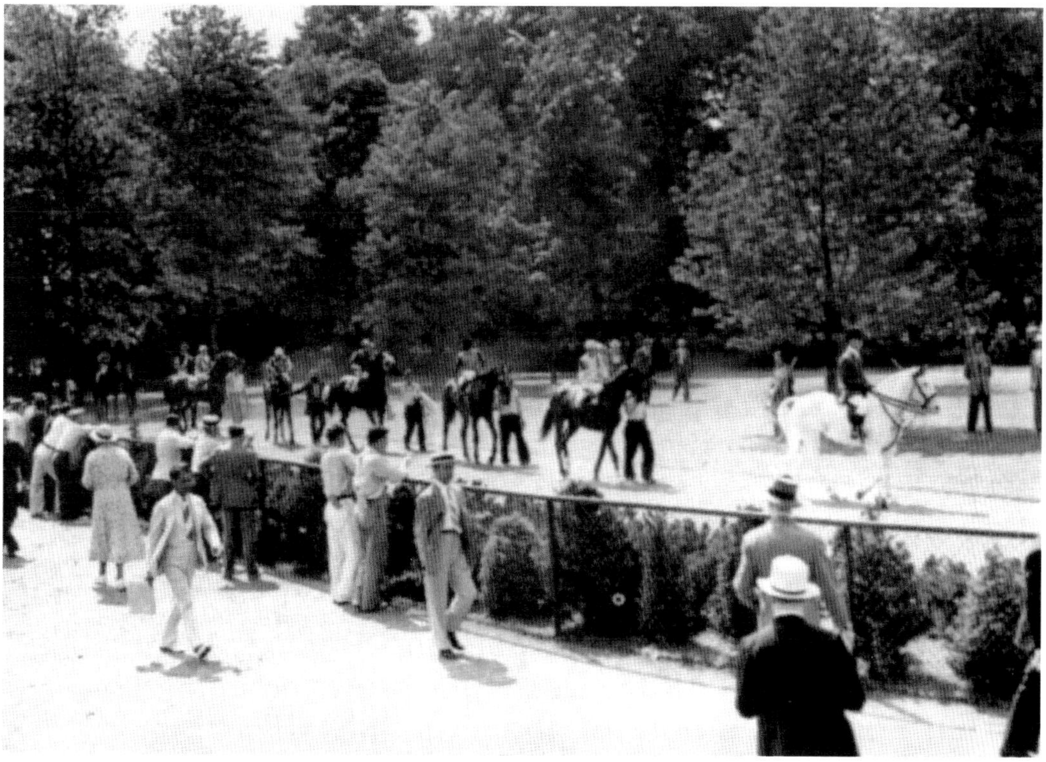

Paddock on opening day, 1937. *Reprinted from the* Saturday Evening Post *magazine, © 1957. Saturday Evening Post Society.*

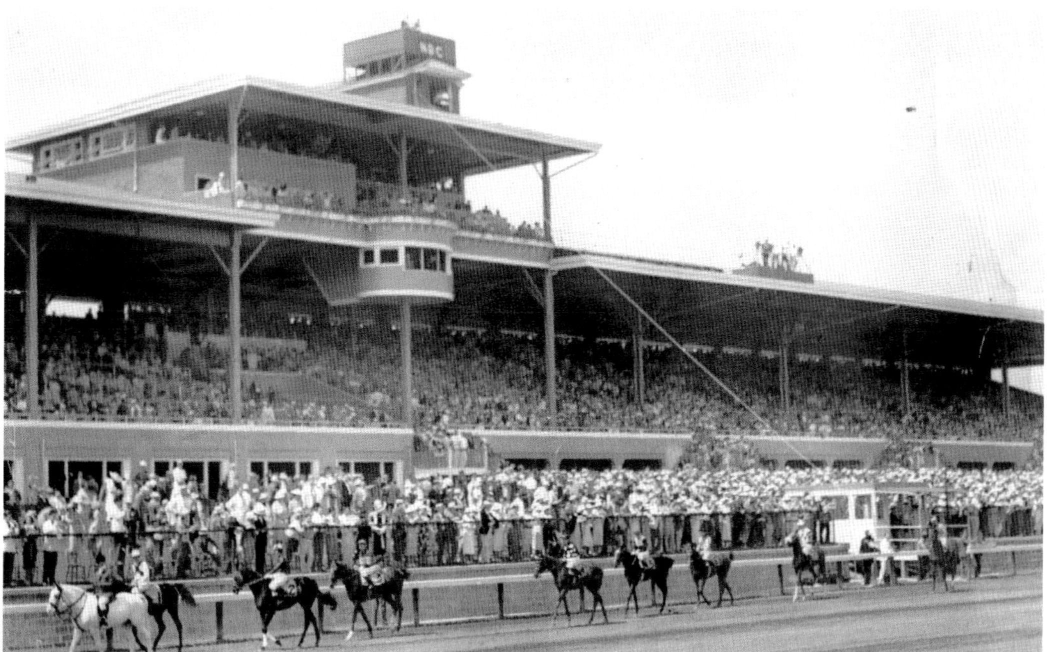

Parade on opening day, June 26, 1937.

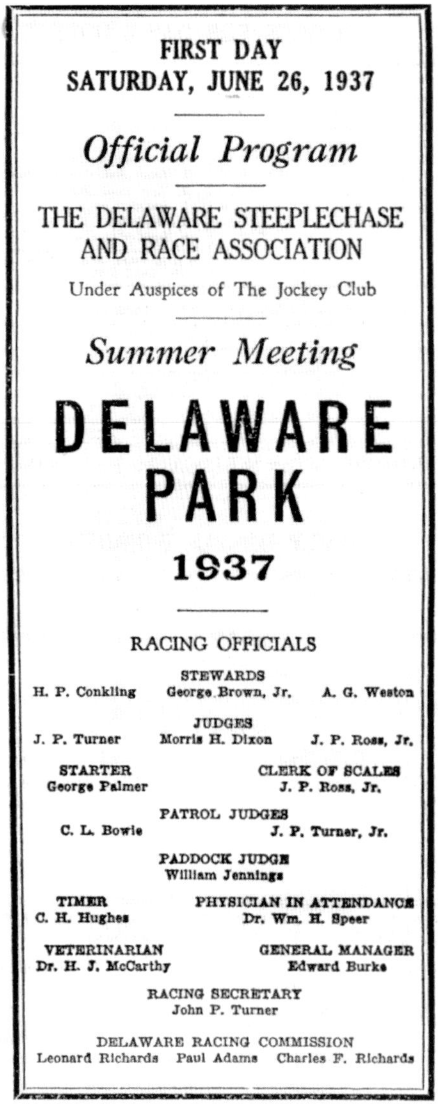

FIRST DAY
SATURDAY, JUNE 26, 1937

Official Program

THE DELAWARE STEEPLECHASE AND RACE ASSOCIATION

Under Auspices of The Jockey Club

Summer Meeting

DELAWARE PARK

1937

RACING OFFICIALS

STEWARDS
H. P. Conkling   George Brown, Jr.   A. G. Weston

JUDGES
J. P. Turner   Morris H. Dixon   J. P. Ross, Jr.

STARTER
George Palmer

CLERK OF SCALES
J. P. Ross, Jr.

PATROL JUDGES
C. L. Bowie   J. P. Turner, Jr.

PADDOCK JUDGE
William Jennings

TIMER
C. H. Hughes

PHYSICIAN IN ATTENDANCE
Dr. Wm. H. Speer

VETERINARIAN
Dr. H. J. McCarthy

GENERAL MANAGER
Edward Burke

RACING SECRETARY
John P. Turner

DELAWARE RACING COMMISSION
Leonard Richards   Paul Adams   Charles F. Richards

Cover of inaugural program, June 26, 1937.

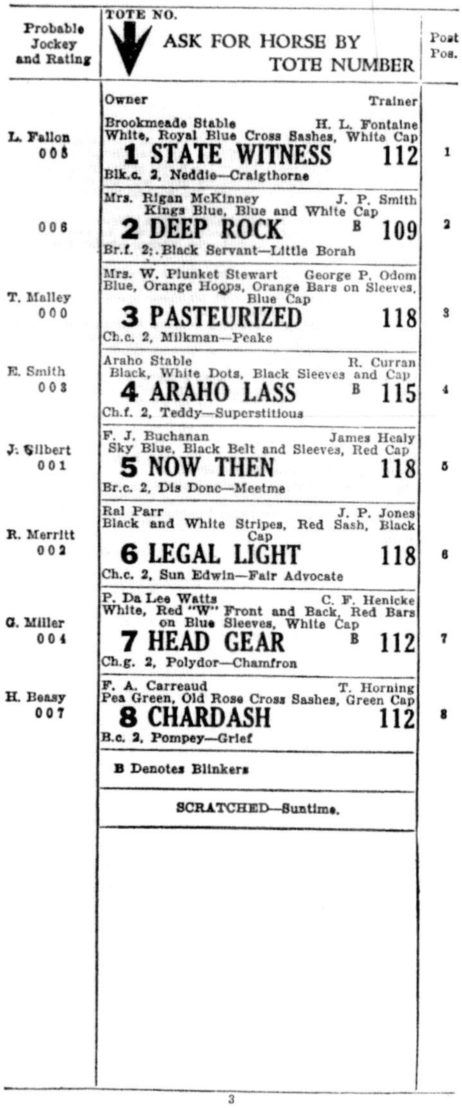

Probable Jockey and Rating	TOTE NO. ASK FOR HORSE BY TOTE NUMBER Owner / Trainer	Post Pos.
L. Fallon 008	Brookmeade Stable — H. L. Fontaine White, Royal Blue Cross Sashes, White Cap **1 STATE WITNESS** 112 Blk.c. 2, Neddie—Craigthorne	1
006	Mrs. Rigan McKinney — J. P. Smith Kings Blue, Blue and White Cap **2 DEEP ROCK** B 109 Br.f. 2, Black Servant—Little Borah	2
T. Malley 000	Mrs. W. Plunket Stewart — George P. Odom Blue, Orange Hoops, Orange Bars on Sleeves, Blue Cap **3 PASTEURIZED** 118 Ch.c. 2, Milkman—Peake	3
E. Smith 003	Araho Stable — R. Curran Black, White Dots, Black Sleeves and Cap **4 ARAHO LASS** B 115 Ch.f. 2, Teddy—Superstitious	4
J. Gilbert 001	F. J. Buchanan — James Healy Sky Blue, Black Belt and Sleeves, Red Cap **5 NOW THEN** 118 Br.c. 2, Dis Donc—Meetme	5
R. Merritt 002	Ral Parr — J. P. Jones Black and White Stripes, Red Sash, Black Cap **6 LEGAL LIGHT** 118 Ch.c. 2, Sun Edwin—Fair Advocate	6
G. Miller 004	P. Da Lee Watts — C. F. Henicke White, Red "W" Front and Back, Red Bars on Blue Sleeves, White Cap **7 HEAD GEAR** B 112 Ch.g. 2, Polydor—Chamfron	7
H. Beasy 007	F. A. Carreaud — T. Horning Pea Green, Old Rose Cross Sashes, Green Cap **8 CHARDASH** 112 B.c. 2, Pompey—Grief	8

B Denotes Blinkers

SCRATCHED—Suntime.

3

Lineup of the first race, June 26, 1937.

The first race at Delaware Park, at 3:00 p.m., was a five-furlong race of two-year-olds. In the field were State Witness, Deep Rock, Pasteurized, Suntime, Araho Lass, Now Then, Legal Light, Head Gear and Chardash. The first race at Delaware Park was won by Legal Light, owned by Ral Parr, who had also won at the Aqueduct the week before. He outpaced the rest of the crowd, passing the five furlongs in one minute even, passing Pasteurized, a son of Milkman, owned by Mrs. Plunkett Stewart, and Now Then, son of Frank Buchanan's Dic Donc.

The feature race of the day was the fifth race, the special $10,000 Kent Handicap race. The favored horse before the race was John Hay Whitney's Flying Scot, winner of the Withers that year at Belmont. Behind Flying Scot was Mrs. C. Oliver Iselin's Strabo, winner of the race at the Aqueduct the previous week, as well as Scrooge; Rex Flag; Pasha, a son of the Porter and Fatima II, owned by Myron Selznick, the California movie producer; Swahill; Jackie D.; Little Sleeper; and Teddy Green. When the bell rang, Flying Scot took the lead and led the race most of the way—he led the backstretch and the turns around the backside. But coming down the homestretch, at the last moment, Mrs. C. Oliver Iselin's Strabo came up on the outside, Jockey Leo Fallon putting on the whip, and Strabo finished the race a half-length ahead in a photo finish for the win. Flying Scot placed second and Rex Flag third. Samuel D. Riddle, watching the race, was confident that had War Admiral been able to run in the race, his horse would have been victorious.[58]

Racing fans experienced a new technology that day, the totalizer. A form of early computer, the machine

> *is the latest mechanical device which had its origins in Australia and has now penetrated England, the Continent, and only last year the United States. As operated in Florida it excludes almost entirely the human element, in addition to arriving at a mathematical result quickly and showing the progress of the betting more accurately.*[59]

Chairman Leonard Richards of the Delaware Racing Commission thought the first day at Delaware Park a brilliant success. He could not see how things could have been better, and his opinion was shared by about everyone else that mattered. The opening day proceeds were considered a great success, with a total of $632,856 wagered. On the Kent Handicap alone, $410,603 was bet.

However, the new racetrack was not without problems. The local press criticized that it was immediately apparent the park was not prepared for the large crowds that it drew. The chief complaint was that the tiered lawn was so high that people standing to watch the races were blocking the views of the patrons on the lower sides of the grandstands. The lawn had been designed originally so that people on it could get a good look at the backstretch, but the benefit of that is negated if the view down the final stretch is blocked.[60]

Another problem with the first rendition of the park was the lack of adequate seating. With the grandstand designed to hold only 7,500 people, the 20,000 who arrived on opening day made for a maddening crush. Patrons who found seating in the grandstand were not willing to move all day, for fear that they would lose their seats. The aisles were packed with people. News reports at the time stated that "it was worth anyone's life to get up and down the aisles. In fact it was impossible because those who had seats or fortunate enough to get standing room refused to move."[61]

On the second day of the meet, with all the opening day festivities over, it rained in the morning so the crowds were smaller and the event was more pleasant. There were no problems with the traffic or parking, and although the track was sloppy, only two scratches were noted.[62] This rain continued for weeks, causing a damper on the early races. About three hundred horses were not let out of the stables for two weeks because

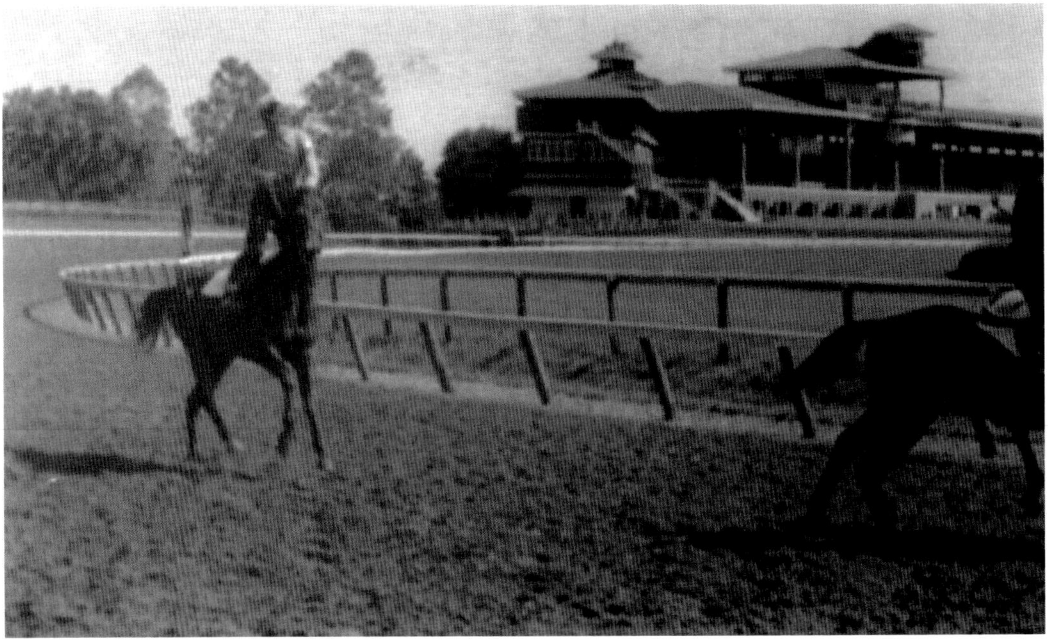

An early photo of Delaware Park.

of unfavorable footing. Those that were allowed to race found the track muddy and slow. A gray and gloomy pallor was cast over the park until the Fourth of July weekend approached.

On June 30, Aneroid, John A. Manfuso's turf sensation, arrived at the park to appear in the $10,000 Brandywine Handicap. He had just been defeated by an eyelash in the Brooklyn Handicap at the Aqueduct by Seabiscuit, the Washington-owned star, but then went on to win at the Suburban Handicap at Belmont. Aneroid had raced seven times in 1937, winning five purses and finishing second and third in the other two, and was the favored horse to win the Brandywine Handicap. Other horses scheduled for the event were G.R. Bryson's Calumet Dick, J.W.Y. Martin's Dark Hope and Mrs. Payne Whitney's Memory Book.[63]

The following weekend was the Fourth of July weekend, and another large crowd was anticipated. Visitors to Wilmington for not only the races but for other planned events began to pack the hotels and restaurants once again. The highlight of the day was the $5,000 Christiana Stakes, a race featuring two-year-olds on a five-and-a-half furlong dash. Favored in the race was C.V. Whitney's Dauber. The sun broke out and the field dried according to its design, and the holiday race was a success.[64]

The next day, however, on July 5, 1937, just weeks after the park was opened, New Castle County was hit with a severe and catastrophic flood. Two men were reported missing (possibly drowned), scores suffered from exposure, more than a hundred families were left homeless, railroad and highway traffic snarled in a nightmarish entanglement and property damage was in the millions in the wake of a severe rainstorm that hit the Newark-Stanton area. The Christiana Creek overtopped its banks and washed out the Cooch's and Chestnut Hill Bridges. Homes on the banks of the Christiana Creek became islands as the creek rose many feet above its normal level, causing furniture and other household belongings to drift out the doors and windows and into the raging torrent. At the village of Christiana, the Christiana Creek rose to eight feet above the bed of the bridge crossing the creek. At Newport, it was ten feet above the flood stage. Hundreds of people in the area were stranded in their cars by the rising waters, unable to proceed anywhere on the flooded roadways, or were forced into available motels and boardinghouses for the evening. Telephone and rail service were also knocked out by the storm.[65]

The epicenter for the storm, at Cooch's Bridge, was only a few miles away from Delaware Park, which also is bounded on the east by the same Christiana Creek. Ten thousand fans were in attendance at the park on the day of the flood. Rain had begun at Delaware Park during the second race of the day, but it wasn't until the horses were going into the barrier for the eighth and final race of the day that the rain turned into a deluge. When the last race was over, fans who had parked their cars on the other side of the underpass and those who held Baltimore and Ohio train tickets found that the underpass was flooded to the top with rainwater.

It took three hours until someone was able to cut a hole in the fence bordering the train tracks, but by then the damage was already done. Much of the parking lot had become a lake, with water rising up to the car seats. Hundreds of cars were stalled, either mired in the mud or their ignition dead from the constant soaking. "An armored car with the tracks and the State's 'cut' of the largest 'take' of the meeting, $439,999, was stuck in the mud but guards surrounded it."[66] Wives and female guests of the drivers huddled under the grandstand for hours while the motorists tried to get their cars free. Food suppliers at the concession stands gave out early and even uncooked hot dogs were at a premium. Even under the grandstand, it was reported that the mud was ankle deep for a time. Still, during the hours that they waited in the grandstand, the marooned crowds kept themselves in good humor with jokes and songs. Women and men took off their shoes and socks and waded around in the warm puddles barefoot. Young men carried their sweethearts the three hundred yards through the mud to the waiting trains.

The most significant damage was to the patrons of the park. Alfred Cleaver of Christiana had to be rescued from a wire fence after his car was washed into the White Clay Creek at Stanton. A woman and five children were stranded in the lunch room in the back of the stable area, where the water had gone up to the height of the tables. At the Trulls' kitchen, where the jockeys had their meals, the flood waters rose to the countertops. At many roadways around the park, those who had successfully left the grounds found that they only got a few miles before their cars were trapped in the flooded roadways or stopped by washed-out bridges, and many ended up spending the night in their cars, or knocking on the doors of private homes and begging for a floor to sleep on. It was reported that some families opened their homes to as many as ten to seventeen of these stranded motorists.

Hundreds of other fans were stranded inside a railroad train for hours because the rain had washed water down from a sloping field onto the Baltimore and Ohio tracks and undermined the spur on which the Philadelphia race train was waiting for the race day to be over. A crew from the Wilsmere yards arrived to pack tons of crushed stone under the rails before the train could proceed. It finally pulled out at 11:20 p.m.

Physical damage to the park itself was limited to only about $2,000, but there was notable damage to the rail lines that serviced it. The lack of transportation caused C.W. Baker, president of the Delaware Steeplechase and Racing Association, to suspend races until the repairs could be exacted. The next day, five hundred men were at work repairing the main line and spurs that had been washed out by the heavy downpour. A water main broke at the stables and water for the horses had to be carried in buckets through the sodden fields.[67]

Partly as a result of the storm, William DuPont Jr. announced a series of improvements to the park before the 1938 season. The grandstand would be extended to twice the size of the original construction. The underpass to the parking lot under the Baltimore and Ohio line would be eliminated and replaced by an overhead bridge. And problems with the view of the track from the clubhouse would have to be corrected as well.[68]

Early meetings experienced, as most early ones do, a dearth of good horses and a plethora of complaints. The Pennsylvania Railroad, which handled heavy passenger traffic between Philadelphia and Washington, ran steam trains to the track, because they had come in on a spur that wasn't electrified. Passengers muscular enough to force open windows in the stifling coaches arrived wearing a veneer of sweaty grime. In the transportation pinch of World War II, the Pennsylvania Railroad dug up even more outdated rolling stock, hermetically sealed express cars in which the passengers were melted down to tallow.

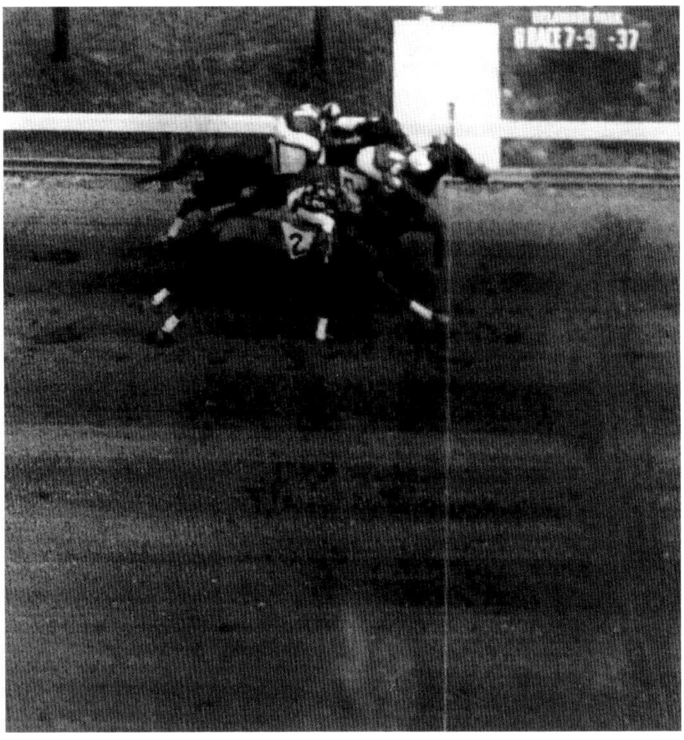

Jones, winner on July 9, 1937.

One of the first notable races occurred at the park soon after the flood. On July 15, the famous horse Man o' War, now seven, was entered into the Greenville Purse, a $1^{1}/_{16}$-mile race. Carrying the blue and gold colors of Mrs. Frank A. Carreaud, who had just signed with the Carreaud outfit, War Glory galloped home five lengths on top after leading every steps of the journey. Some eight thousand fans saw War Glory score his triumph. The track was slow at the time of the feature, due to overnight rains.[69]

Understandably, the first set of track records were set in 1937. The Wheatly Stable's Merry Lassie, owned by Mrs. H.C. Phipps and her brother, Ogden L. Mills, ran one of the fastest five furlongs of any track to date, when it ran $59^{1}/_{5}$ in the \$5,000 Polly Drummond Stakes. William DuPont's Rosenna set the mark for $1^{1}/_{16}$-mile race in the New Castle Handicap, with a pace of $1{:}43^{4}/_{5}$. And notably, the only horse to win two stakes at the park in that first year was Mrs. C. Oliver Iselin's three-year old Strabo, who took the \$10,000 Kent Handicap on opening day and the \$7,500 Diamond State Handicap. The initial year's set of records were as follows:[70]

1937 Records

5 Furlongs	Wheatly Stables Merry Lassie	$59^{1}/_{5}$
$5^{1}/_{2}$ Furlongs	Ral Parr's Legal Light	$1.06^{2}/_{5}$
6 Furlongs	Mrs. W.P. Stewart's Mower	$1.11^{3}/_{5}$
Mile & 70 yards	W.E. Johnson's Icy Wind	$1.43^{1}/_{5}$
Mile & $^{1}/_{16}$	William duPont Jr.'s Rosenna	$1.43^{4}/_{5}$
Mile & $^{1}/_{8}$	Mrs. C. Oliver Iselin's Strabo	$1.53^{2}/_{5}$
Mile & $^{1}/_{4}$	E.K. Bryson's Calumet Dick	$2.04^{1}/_{5}$

All told, the inaugural year of Delaware Park was a great success. At the conclusion of the meet, Charles W. Baler, president of the Delaware Steeplechase and Race Association, announced that \$6,300,000 was wagered in its opening year. Tax revenue to the state, into desperate coffers, amounted to approximately \$225,000. The greatest attendance for the meet was put at about twenty thousand, on July 5 of that year. Baker commented that a part of the profits from the first year would be turned into improvements at the track, "for the convenience and comfort of our patrons. Plans are being formulated for next year, which should increase not only the number, but the quality of our entries."[71]

After the racing was over and the horses all returned to their home farms, the management began to initiate \$50,000 worth of improvements to the park, some in response to the problems that had arisen in 1937. Improvements included an overhead bridge to cross the railroad tracks, to alleviate the problems caused when the tunnel flooded during the previous year, and the construction of more "slope" to the lawn so that patrons could see the entire racetrack. Also included in the modifications were additional seats in the grandstand, increased space under shelter from the weather and additional barns for the horsemen. The park also completed work on the steeplechase course into the center of the track, one to rival those at Woodbine, Belmont and Saratoga. Although the course had been laid out for its inaugural year, an additional year was needed for the grass to mature and thicken properly. It was planned that jumping events would be held daily, if horses could be arranged.[72]

At the opening of the twenty-eight-day 1938 meet, the big news was that a number of important Pennsylvania stables would be represented this year. Baker's promise of increasing the quality of the racing at the park was coming true. Enlisted for the 1938 meet were the stables of George D. Widener, Mr. and Mrs. Walter M. Jeffords, Mrs. W. Plunkett Stewart and Elmer Dale Shaffer. Widener's Erdenheim Stables, at Chestnut Hill in Philadelphia, were famous as the birthplace of Iroquois, son of Leamington and Maggie B.B., the only American horse to win an English Derby at that time. Their horse, Salamis, was considered a favorite before the racing started.

Expecting a good season as well, columnist Rutledge commented:

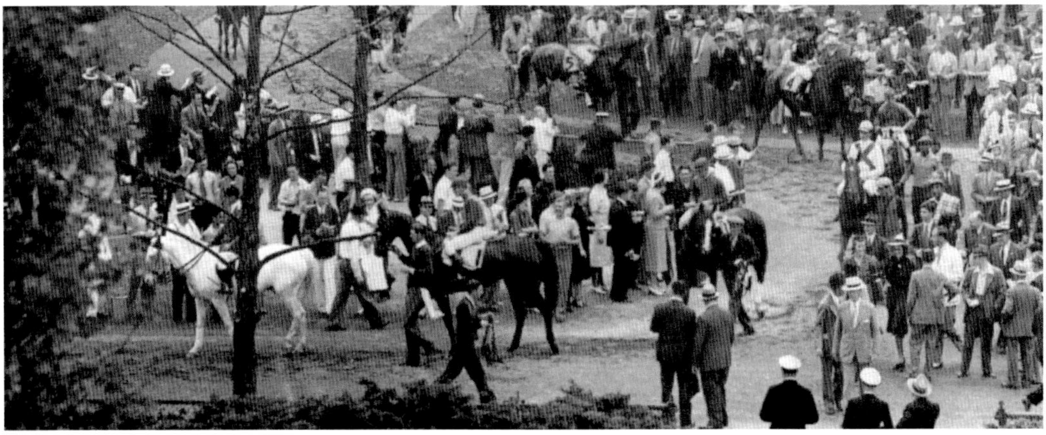

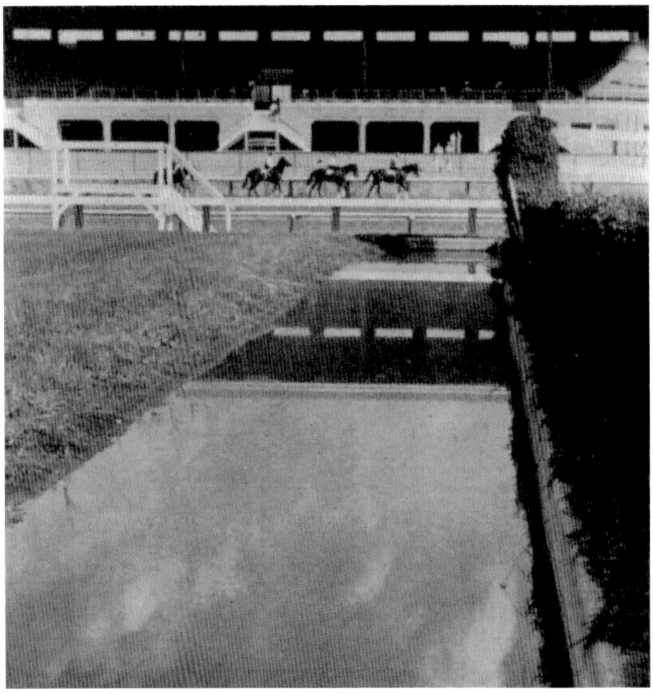

Above: Walking the steeplechasing horses at Delaware Park, 1949. *From* Steeplechasing, *Thayer, 1949.*

Left: The water jump at Delaware Park. *From* Steeplechasing, *Thayer, 1949.*

> *America loves a gamble and people in the Diamond State are thoroughly American in every respect. How the money is accumulated isn't important. The desire to gamble is deep-rooted in human beings. They gather the money to satisfy that desire somewhere, somehow. Possibly a meal is missed, but John Q. Public thinks nothing of a gnawing in his belly providing a good thing is running at the track. He's a gambler at heart and loves to pursue the will-o-the-wisp offered by juicy daily doubles, platers kicking home ahead of stakes horses at odds of 1000 to 1, and other attractions he knows as possibilities. He doesn't consider improbabilities, nor consequences. Recession or no recession, Delaware Park's forthcoming meet lines up as a success in every respect by which such events are measured.*[73]

William DuPont swelled with pride the following year when his horse, Dauber, received national attention. A grandson of Man o' War, Dauber won the $69,000 Preakness Stakes, the richest race for three-year-old thoroughbreds that year. Through the rain and mist, twenty-five thousand dripping spectators watched Dauber start unostentatiously, as a well-mannered Whitney colt would be expected to do. But going into the backstretch, Dauber began to make a spectacle of himself—not in front, but trailing behind (in next to last place in the field of nine), ten lengths in back of the leaders, Menow and Fighting Fox. Gloom settled over the stands. Even stretch-running Dauber could never make up that distance. Suddenly a roar went up, "Look at Dauber!" The DuPont colt had suddenly started to flash past the horses in front of him as though they were telegraph poles. He overtook them one by one, splashing mud in their blinkered faces, and finished seven lengths in front of the tired crop of three-year-olds who found the 1³/16-mile too long a distance.

The runner-up was Cravat, a former stable mate of Dauber's in the Whitney string, who had been twenty lengths behind the leaders at the half-mile post and had made an equally astonishing stretch finish. Pace-setting Menow was third and Can't Wait was fourth. Dauber's victory was worth $51,875 and brought his 1938 winnings to $69,175, second only to those of Stagehand. Owner DuPont already had a neat profit on the chestnut colt he had bought from Cornelius Vanderbilt Whitney for $29,000.[74] Later that year, Dauber went on to finish second in the $60,000 Santa Anita Derby, after finishing second to Lawrin in the $57,000 Kentucky Derby and then winning the Preakness.

Another of the early notables was famous jockey Eddie Arcaro (February 16, 1916–November 4, 1997). This Hall of Fame jockey won his first Kentucky Derby in 1938 on Lawrin, and went on to win the Triple Crown twice, on Whirlaway in 1941 and on Citation in 1948. Arcaro raced an astounding 24,092 races and won a total of 4,779 of them.[75]

Eddie Arcaro's racing was always a favorite during the early days at Delaware Park. In 1940, under a perfectly judged ride by Eddie Arcaro, Piquet, the speedy daughter of St. Germans and Parry, raced past the judges one length before G.D. Widener's Rosetown when she came from far back to win the fourth running of the $4,000 added Delaware Oaks. The Foxcatcher Farms' Fairy Chant earned third money by a length over Hal Price Headley's Salaminis. In addition to top money, trainer John M. Gaver also accepted a handsome trophy from Miss Alice Marble, women's national tennis champion, who made the presentation on behalf of the Delaware Steeplechase and Race Association.[76]

THE WAR YEARS

No hour of life is lost that is spent in the saddle.
—Winston Churchill

Delaware during World War II was an important center of industrial activity for the war effort. It was situated in the "vital triangle" of industry, bounded by New York, Pittsburgh and Norfolk. The Wilmington shipyards, especially the works of the Dravo Corporation, launched hundreds of merchant vessels to the Christiana River during wartime production. The chemical facilities at the works of DuPont, Hercules and Atlas were critical in the supply of gunpowder. The state's iron and steel foundries, textiles manufacturers and other industries were all at full production during the time. The heavy industries brought thousands of new residents to Wilmington, and the city greatly increased in size as a result. And many of them eventually discovered Delaware Park as a place to rest from their important toils.

Delaware Park management always seemed willing to accommodate everyone and to try new things. As trouble brewed around the world, the last summer of peace at Delaware Park was highlighted by continued improvements. Always interested in keeping the racing fun, in 1941 Delaware Park began to put little cartoons on their Daily Double tickets. There was even a cream soda that was manufactured in Philadelphia and sold at the park!

Responding to complaints that there were not enough stalls for horses there, in 1941 they announced a "taxi service for several hundred horses stabled at nearby Fair Hill, providing vans for service between the farms and the Park."[77] The several hundred horses were stabled at Fair Hill, Maryland, from where a fleet of vans, each carrying six horses, could provide service to the farms and the track.[78]

The racing business was welcomed by the community and the sport flourished. William DuPont's stable reached its pinnacle at this time, having Staretor placing second at the Kentucky Derby in 1941 and Fairy Manah placing thirteenth in 1942 at the same race.

As the war dragged on, the crisis of supplies in almost every industry began to take its toll. Unfortunately, in April of 1942 it became evident that the impact of the war would

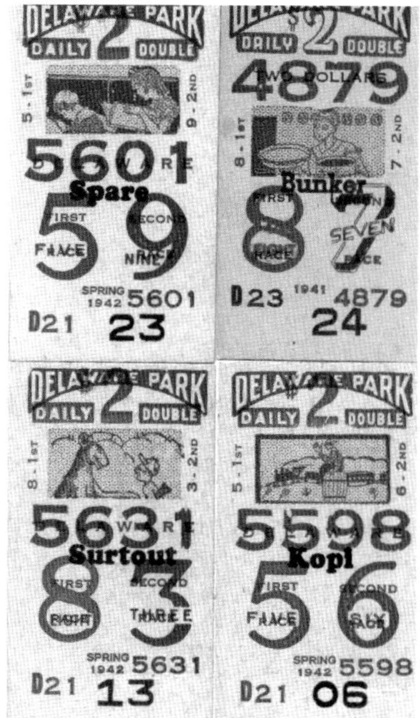

Right: 1942 race tickets with little cartoons.

Below: 1940s Delaware Park Cream Soda label.

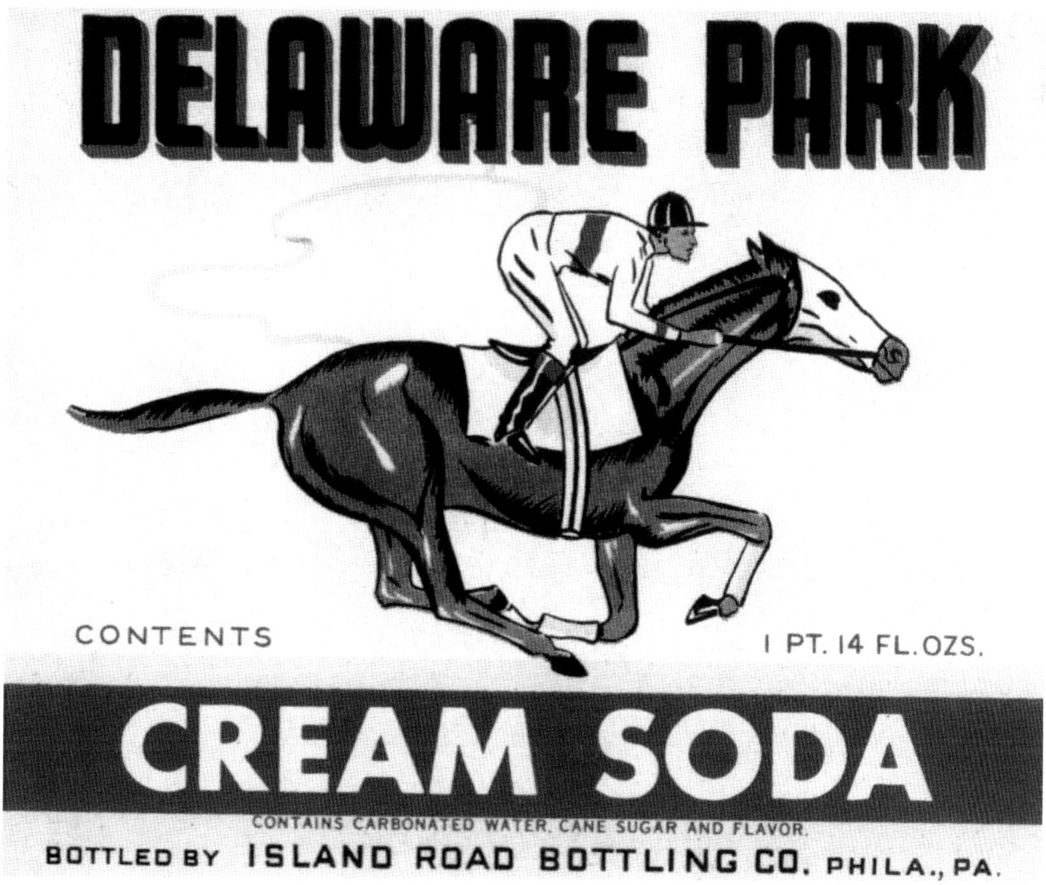

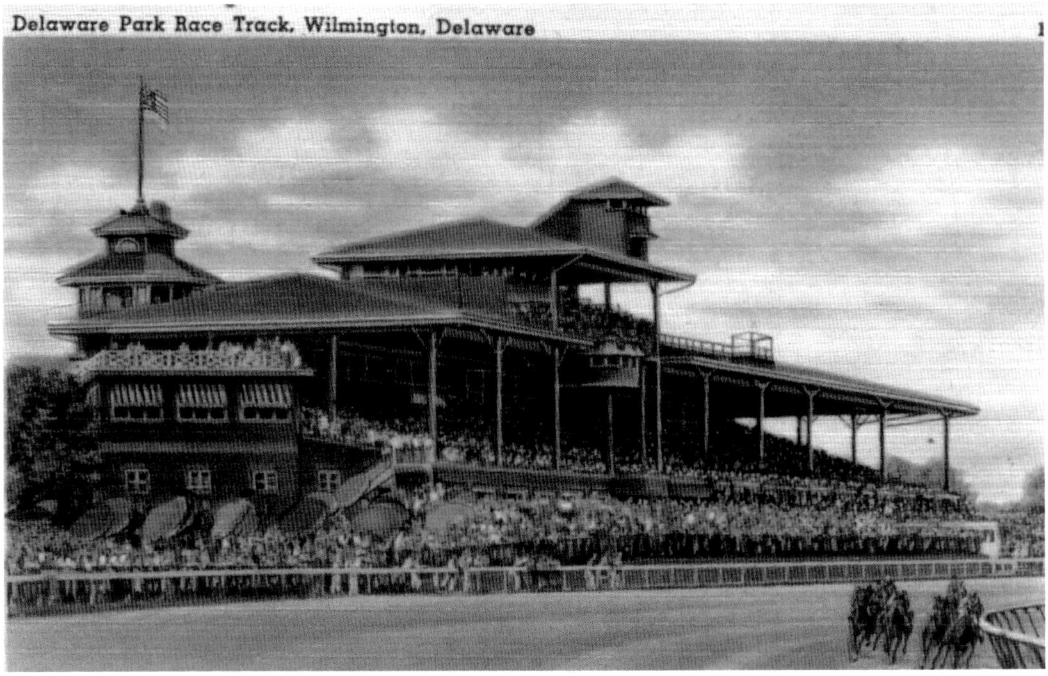

1940s postcard.

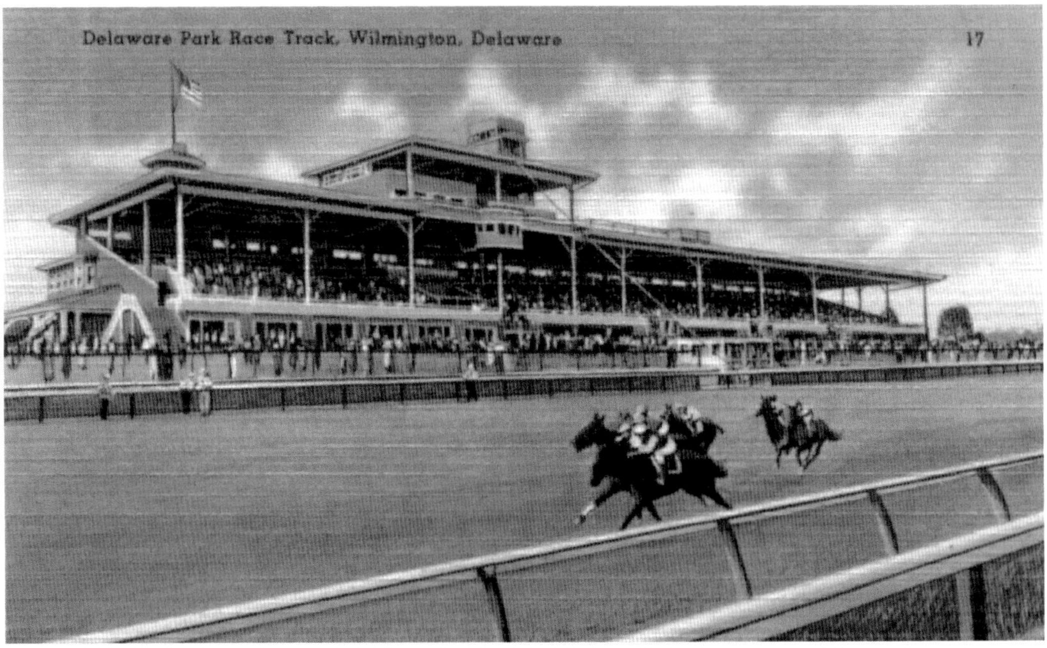

1940s postcard.

be felt at Delaware Park as well. President Roosevelt conducted a radio address to the nation, expressing concerns that there was not enough of a supply of rubber to support the war effort. *Time* magazine reported that the president told the nation:

> *I want to talk to you about rubber—about rubber and the war—about rubber and the American people. Rubber was a problem, said Mr. Roosevelt, because 92% of our normal supply had been cut off by the Japanese. The shortage would be even more serious if we had not built up a "huge stockpile" and if we were not now building up a great new synthetic-rubber industry. But neither stockpile nor synthetic "both together will be enough to provide for the needs of our great new Army and Navy plus our civilian requirements as they now exist." He designated a two-week period (June 15–30) in which to get all the old rubber in "where it can stand up and be counted." For all rubber that citizens salvaged from cellars and attics, gas-station operators would pay 1¢ per pound. The Government will pay them back. Then, said Mr. Roosevelt, "We will make our plans…One thing you can be sure of—we are going to see to it that there is enough rubber to build the planes to bomb Tokyo and Berlin—enough rubber to build the tanks to crush the enemy wherever we may find him—enough rubber to win the war."*[79]

The connection between the supply of rubber on a national level and its impact on Delaware Park is not immediately evident. Because of the demands on the railroads for wartime use, all rail transportation to the track was suspended. Therefore, the only way that fans could get to the track was by automobile; before the development of the interstate transportation system, the only avenue to the park was over long, poorly maintained roadways. To reduce the amount of rubber consumed by the general public for what was considered entertainment, rubber director William Jeffers personally requested that horse racing tracks like Delaware Park close until the crisis was over. The directors of the Delaware Steeplechase and Racing Association consented, and originally planned to suspend racing until the 1944 season.[80]

Thankfully, the rubber crisis abated by the end of the year. The 1943 season was originally begun with an apprehensive hope. William DuPont Jr., who was in town for a meeting, told reporters that Delaware Park had every expectation of staging a 1943 meeting at Stanton, Delaware. He gave out a formal statement by the executive committee, of which he was a member. The other committee members were Donald P. Ross, also a Jockey Club member, and President J. Simpson Dean, then a captain in the Air Force.[81]

In its 1944 season, Delaware Park became profitable, with a handle of more than $23 million from 288,000 customers. Even though the war raged on and times were generally tough, it was noted that by the first of June, there was "no sign of a let-up in the increased attendance and handle at Delaware Park…as 5869 fans came to the track."[82] The first notable event of that year was the appointment of a new general manager, Byran Field, a New York turf writer, because of Edward Burke's ill health.[83]

At the time, Byran Field was a racing writer for the *New York Times*. Born and raised in New York, somewhere he developed an Oxford accent that became familiar to fans

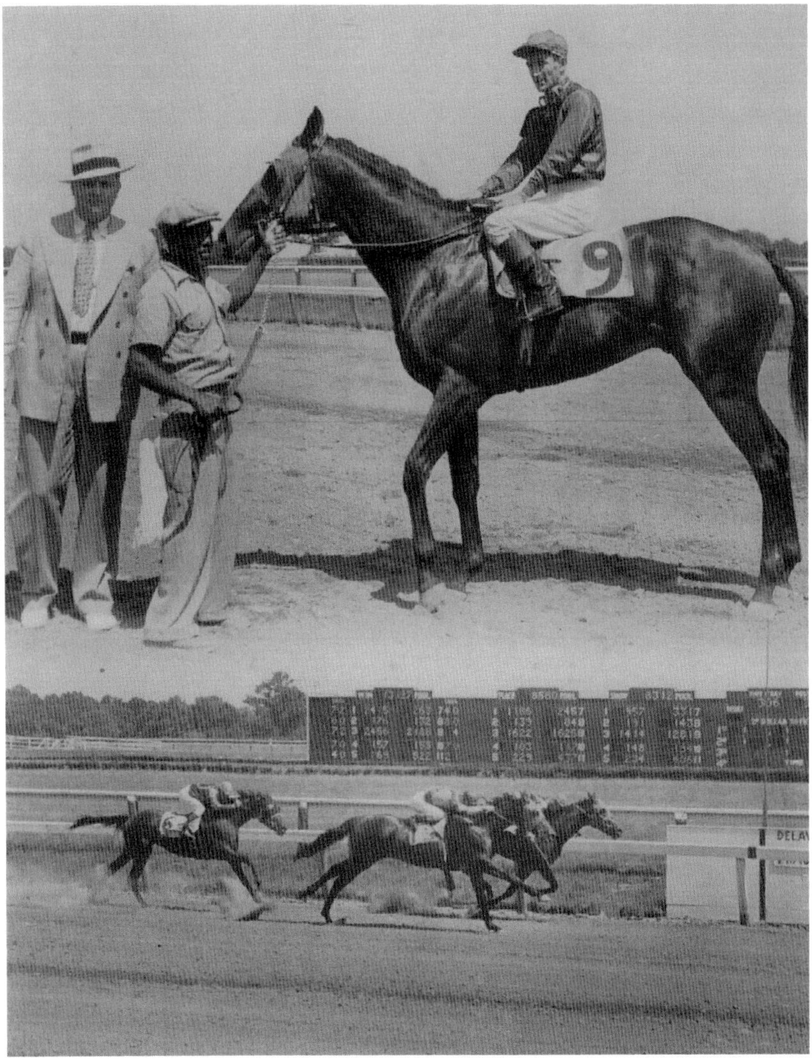

Winner's circle photo of Valdina Bien, June 16, 1942. R. Sisto up, trained by J.H. Logan.

at the New York tracks via loudspeaker, and to radio listeners who tuned in to hear such events as the Kentucky Derby. When Field was offered the position of general manager at Delaware Park, he was reluctant to give up his other jobs in New York. He enlisted the help of a friend, Fred Capossela, who imitated him on the radio so Field could escape to the train to get to Delaware Park for his job there. He decided to quit his job at the *Times* in 1944, and soon left all the announcing to Capossela so he could concentrate on his duties in Delaware.[84]

By the summer of 1944, it was evident that the war was going to be drawing to a close soon. As the federal government announced D-Day in June, most of the tracks around the country decided to forego racing events, but not Delaware Park. The owners decided to buck the national trend and provide racing as a benefit to the war effort. All profits from the special D-Day program, estimated at $51,000, as well as jockey fees, were to be contributed

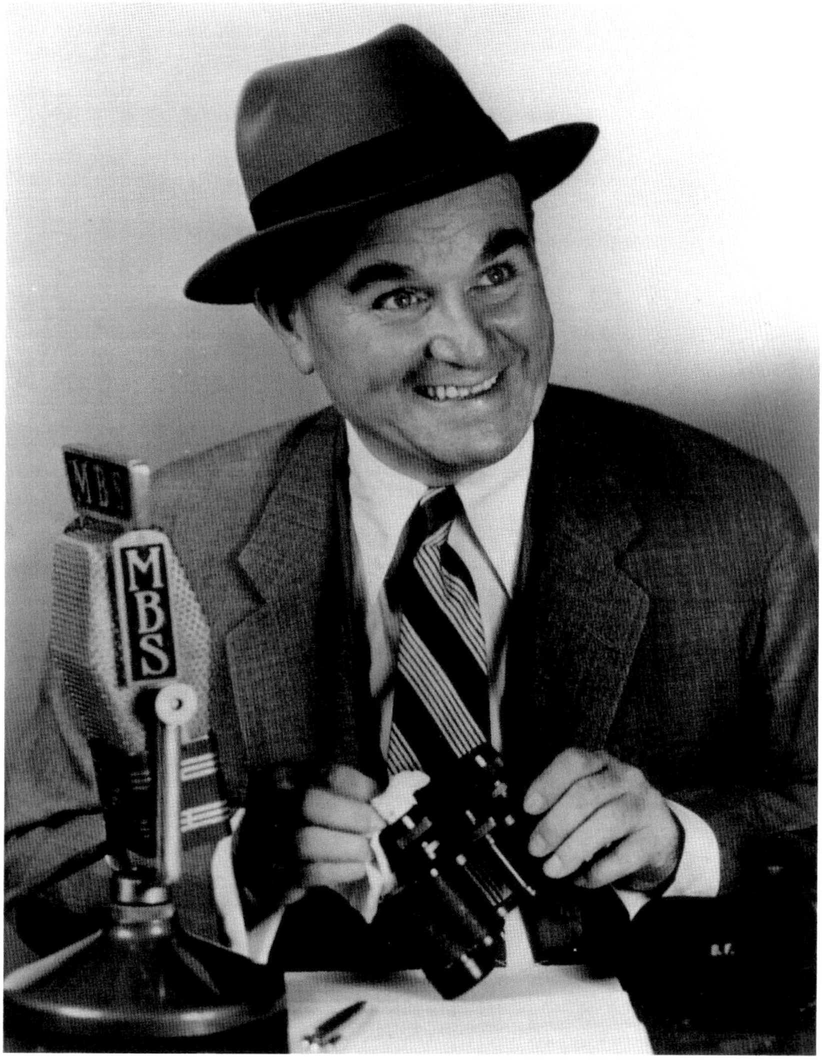

Byran Field, longtime general manager at Delaware Park.

to the Red Cross and United Service Organization, the management announced. Byran Field, general manager of the track, issued the following statement: "Delaware Park on this grave day announces its war bond distribution to horsemen, and purses will be increased 50 per cent—all in war bonds. It was decided that closing our race on D-Day wouldn't help, but that carrying on would help. We are working and carrying on."

An hour or so before the first race the jockeys were in colors, but upon word from the Jockeys Community Fund and Guild Headquarters in New York that riders elsewhere were not plying their trade, they asked for a conference with General Manager Field. A committee headed by Nick Wall waited on Field and later the general manager spoke to all riders in the jockey room. Torn between their loyalty to the Guild and their obvious opportunity to contribute materially to the war effort, the jockeys were in long consultation before deciding to accept mounts.[85]

The Glory Years

No one can teach riding so well as a horse.
–C.S. Lewis

The glory years at Delaware Park began with the formal end of World War II and continued into the 1960s. America was at peace again, and the soldiers came home to their loved ones and started new families. Construction began on the Delaware Memorial Bridge in 1951, finally providing access from New Jersey. Population increased by 40 percent throughout the state. Major automobile manufacturers built plants in Elsmere and Newark, and the beginnings of suburban development began to carve up the fallow fields in New Castle County and place houses upon them.

The year 1947 marked the emergence of one of the greatest horses of all time, the noted Citation. Born and bred at Calumet Farm in Lexington, Kentucky, to Bull Lea and Hydroplane, Citation won his first race as a two-year-old at Havre de Grace, and won nine times after his first win, a total of $155,680. In 1948 Citation, ridden by Eddie Arcaro, went on to win the Triple Crown and Horse of the Year honors. He won the Kentucky Derby by three and a half lengths, the Preakness by five and a half lengths and then the Belmont. He continued racing until 1951, becoming the first horse to win $1 million. After retiring, Citation lived a long, peaceful life on his home farm, siring Hall of Famer Silver Spoon and 1956 Preakness winner Fabius. In 1959, he was inducted into the National Museum of Racing and Hall of Fame. Citation died on August 8, 1970.[86]

The longest standing record at the park was recorded on June 26, 1948, a record that has survived almost sixty years. The gathering of 16,657 fans in a picture-perfect day at the park watched as Mill River Stable's Bam, who couldn't get up a good gallop in the Kiamanski Handicap the week before, surprised the crowd with lightning. Running under Conn McCreary, Bam found a fast track and established the new track record at 2:31 for one and a half miles, ahead by three lengths of Lawndale Stable's Alacrity and Henry L. Straus's Pilaster.

At that time, Delaware Park attempted to expand its interest and revenue sources by adding boxing to the fare. A boxing ring was set up under the grandstand and fights

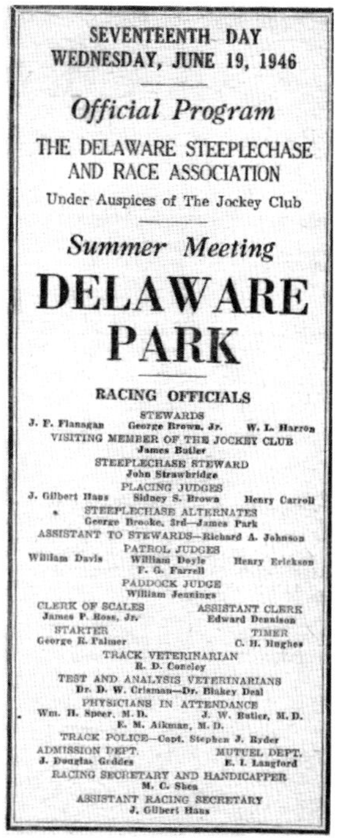

SEVENTEENTH DAY
WEDNESDAY, JUNE 19, 1946

Official Program

THE DELAWARE STEEPLECHASE AND RACE ASSOCIATION

Under Auspices of The Jockey Club

Summer Meeting

DELAWARE PARK

RACING OFFICIALS

STEWARDS
J. F. Flanagan — George Brown, Jr. — W. L. Harron

VISITING MEMBER OF THE JOCKEY CLUB
James Butler

STEEPLECHASE STEWARD
John Strawbridge

PLACING JUDGES
J. Gilbert Haas — Sidney S. Brown — Henry Carroll

STEEPLECHASE ALTERNATES
George Brooke, 3rd—James Park

ASSISTANT TO STEWARDS—Richard A. Johnson

PATROL JUDGES
William Davis — William Doyle — Henry Erickson
F. G. Farrell

PADDOCK JUDGE
William Jennings

CLERK OF SCALES
James P. Ross, Jr.

ASSISTANT CLERK
Edward Dennison

STARTER
George R. Palmer

TIMER
C. H. Hughes

TRACK VETERINARIAN
R. D. Coneley

TEST AND ANALYSIS VETERINARIANS
Dr. D. W. Crisman—Dr. Blakey Deal

PHYSICIANS IN ATTENDANCE
Wm. H. Speer, M. D. — J. W. Butler, M. D.
E. M. Aikman, M. D.

TRACK POLICE—Capt. Stephen J. Ryder

ADMISSION DEPT.
J. Douglas Geddes

MUTUEL DEPT.
E. I. Langford

RACING SECRETARY AND HANDICAPPER
M. C. Shea

ASSISTANT RACING SECRETARY
J. Gilbert Haas

Right: Program, 1946 session.

Below: Citation, circa 1947, Eddie Arcaro up.

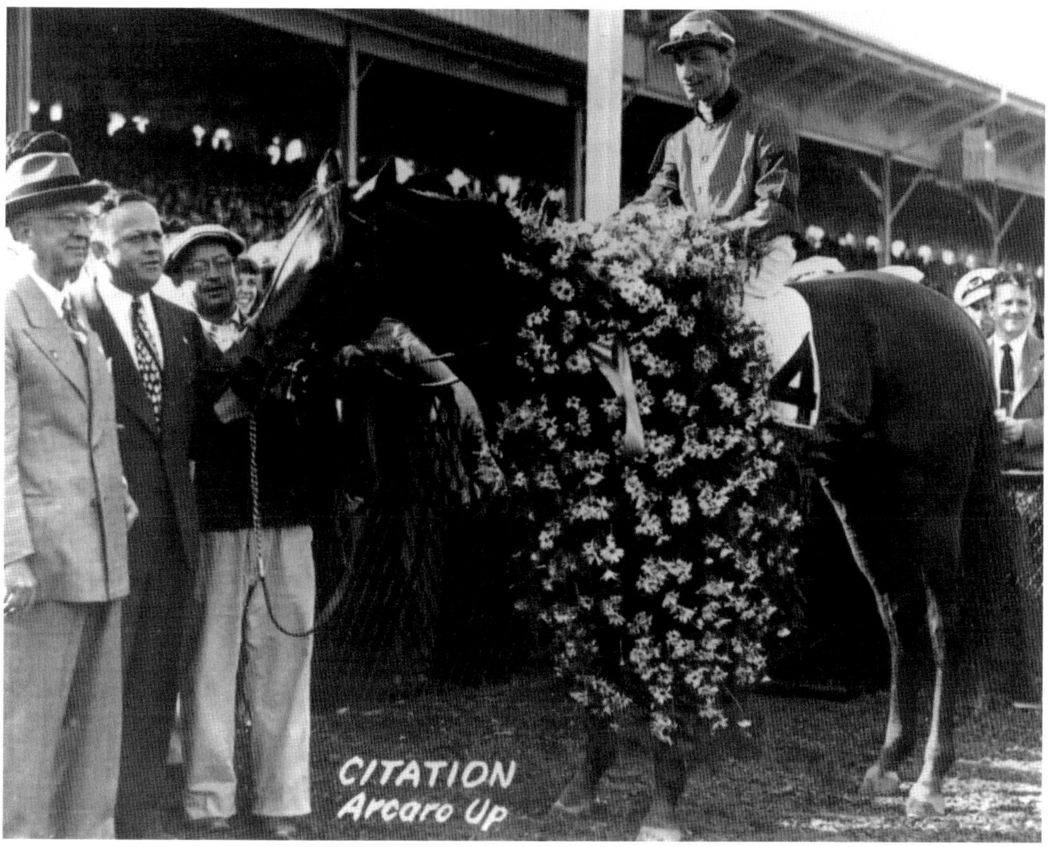

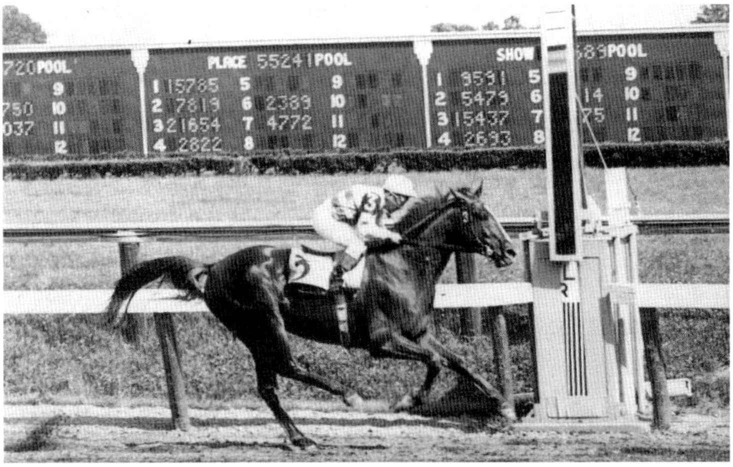

Mrs. Ethel D. Jacobs's Stymie wins the 1947 Sussex Handicap.

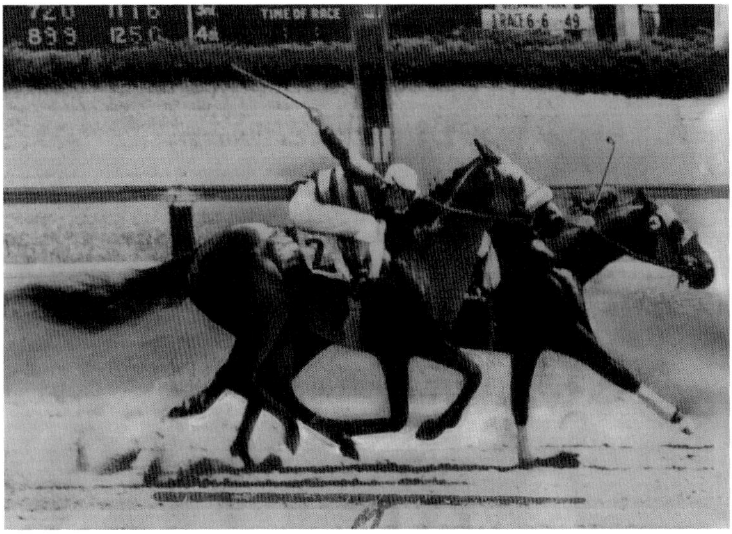

Vim Lives, winner on June 7, 1949; Willie Downs up.

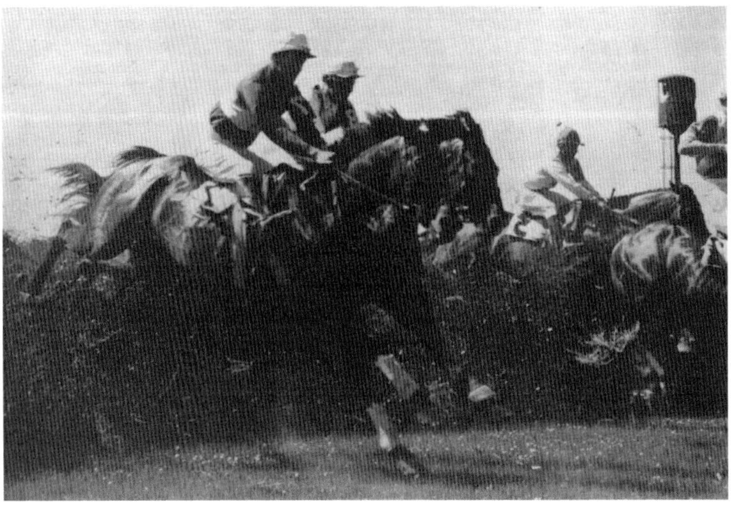

Brookmeade Stables' His Boots, winning the 1949 Tom Roby Stakes. *From* Steeplechasing, *Thayer, 1949.*

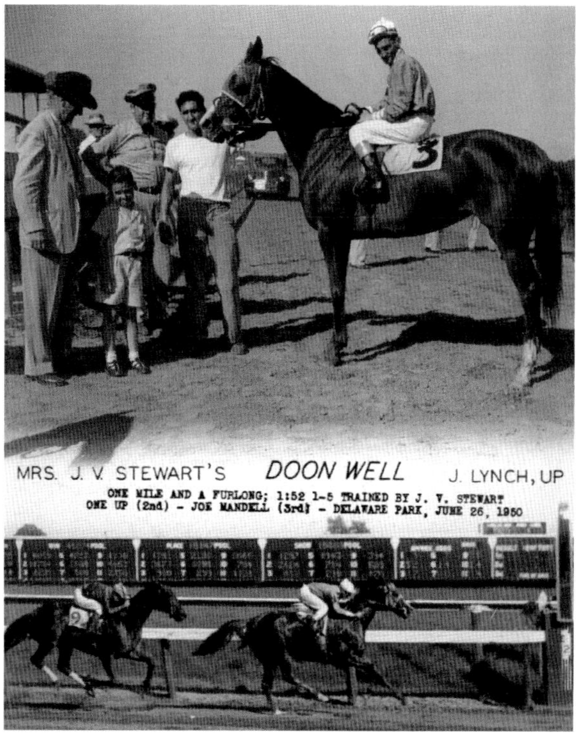

Doon Well, winner on June 26, 1950. Mrs. J.V. Stewart, owner, J. Lynch, up.

were held in the evenings. Another innovation occurred on May 7, 1949, when Calumet Farm's Ponder won the seventy-fifth Kentucky Derby, which was first telecast on a limited basis by local television station WAVE. On May 3, 1952, the first coast-to-coast, network-televised Kentucky Derby aired on CBS. Favorite Hill Gail won the Derby, giving his jockey Eddie Arcaro a record fifth victory in the Kentucky Derby, and his trainer, Ben A. Jones, the record for most wins (six). Arcaro's record was matched on that day in 1969 by jockey Bill Hartack. Jones's record has not been equaled.[87]

Delaware Park opened for a new session on May 29, 1951, with the first daily double since the park closed for the war in 1942. It featured a new invention: "Credited to Track superintendent Clarke M. Pardee is what he believes to be the only hydraulically-powered odds board, which will display the possible double payoff figures and be raised and lowered between the early races, causing no view obstructed during the actual races." The season attracted some of the most important horses on the East Coast, including Mrs. W.M. Jerrords's 1950 winner Adile, Alfred G. Vanderbilt's Next Move, King Ranch's Renew and Foxcatcher Farms' Gallery. Opening day featured the $10,000, six-furlong Delaware Handicap and two events named after the American Legion and the Veterans of Foreign Affairs. For these two latter races, several thousand veterans were honored guests, and special celebrations were held for their service to American freedom.[88]

The second longest record at Delaware Park was set on June 27, 1951. In the sixth race, Keystone Stable's Cer Vantes was ridden by Ronald Nash and was thought to be off the pace at the onset. Quemadito, who had already won the fourth race that day,

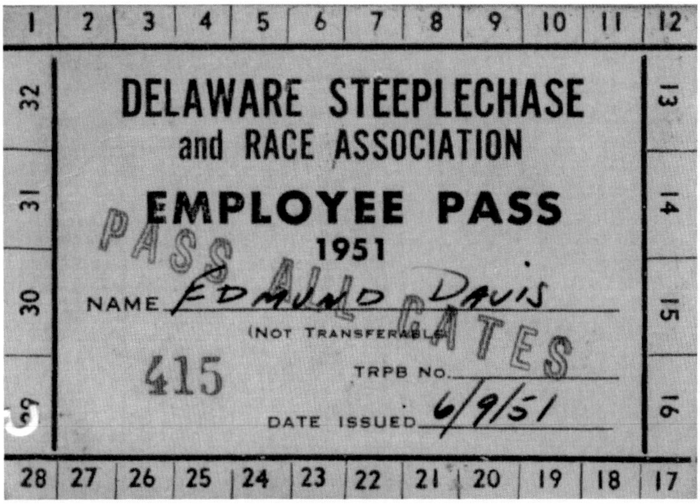

1951 employee pass of Edmund Davis.

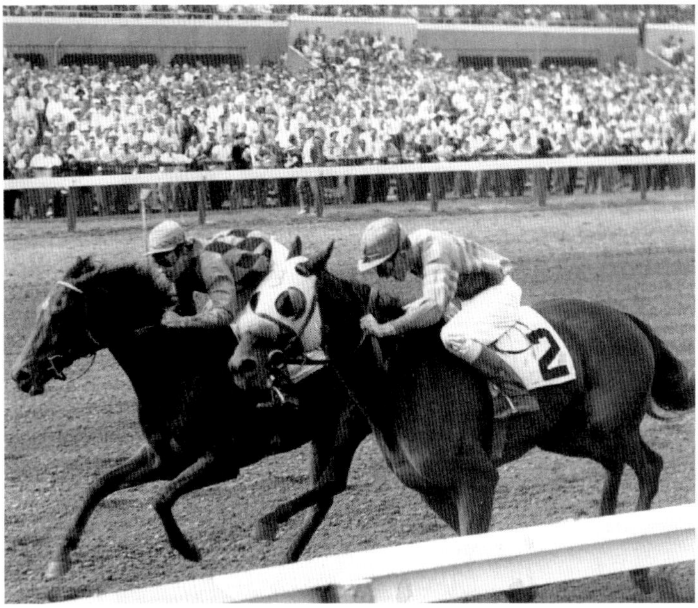

Vital, winning on June 6, 1951, Doyle Gardner up.

was considered the favorite, but he trailed in the race. Cer Vantes breezed past Jitters and finished the race ahead by seven lengths. In doing so, he set the record for one and three-quarters miles, at 2:56.40; this record is still standing. Right after Cer Vantes was off the field, a violent storm hit the park, uprooting trees in the paddock![89]

Byran Field, as general manager, operated the park with a close hand through the 1950s. Field discovered early that when a man says he is running a nonprofit enterprise, he doesn't mean an unprofitable one. Generally speaking, rich men do not abhor money, even if they don't covet more. The general manager was expected to keep Delaware in the black, but not too much in the black. If Field had a meeting of thirty-three days—the original thirty-day limit had been relaxed by law to work in holiday programs on

Memorial Day and July Fourth—he split it into three parts. Business done in the first eleven days, and in the second eleven, helped him estimate how much money to give away in purses in the last eleven, so that he wouldn't get stuck with a lot of extra money.

In 1955 there was about $102,000 left over; in 1956 there was only $80,000 or so. Maintaining this delicate balance was not necessarily made easier by the detached view of the sordid side that was taken by Field's bosses. Once the stewards excused an injured favorite that was going to the post carrying $36,000 in wagers, but they let the race start before a refund had been arranged. The payoff would have to be computed with the $36,000 in the pool. Hastily, Field consulted Don Ross, the president: How about the people who had bet the favorite? "Give 'em their money back," Ross said. Paying out $36,000 in house funds, the general manager winced at this bite in his budget. The next day he howled, for the racing commission was around demanding the state's tax on the $36,000 he'd given away.

Famous horses attracted customers and frightened away competition. Tracks dread small fields and "minus pools," in which there are not enough losing bets to make up the minimum legal payoff to the winners. Delaware seldom varied the policy of accepting win-place-show bets if as many as four horses start. During one race, the good mare Cerise Reine was a stick-out in a small field that was reduced to six starters when it came up mud after a heavy rain. "Take bets across the board," Ross instructed. Then another horse was scratched because of injury. Field sought out the president again. "I thought we had that all settled," Ross said. "But," Field protested, "that was before this other horse was scratch—Oh, well, it's your money."[90]

Delaware Park, with its prime location, became a haven for summer racing fans throughout the middle Atlantic region. Trainloads of race goers came via the Baltimore and Ohio and Pennsylvania Railroads to the trackside terminals. Scores of buses rolled in daily from Washington, Baltimore, Philadelphia and New York. Crowds of more than twenty thousand were commonplace on Saturdays.

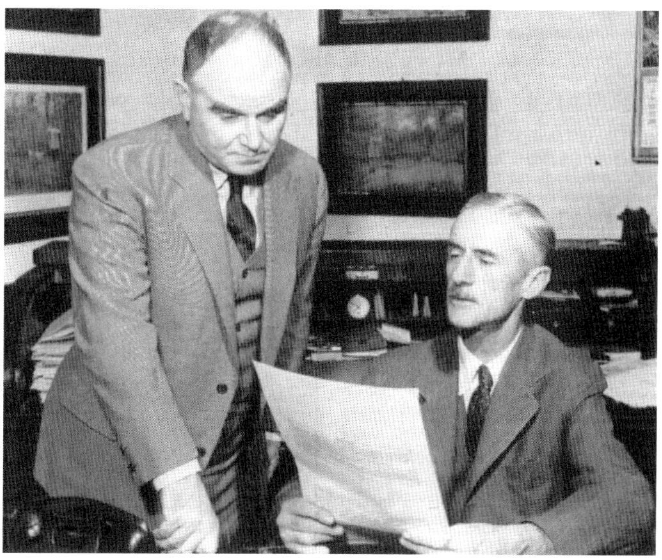

William DuPont and Byran Fields. *Reprinted from the* Saturday Evening Post *magazine, © 1957. Saturday Evening Post Society.*

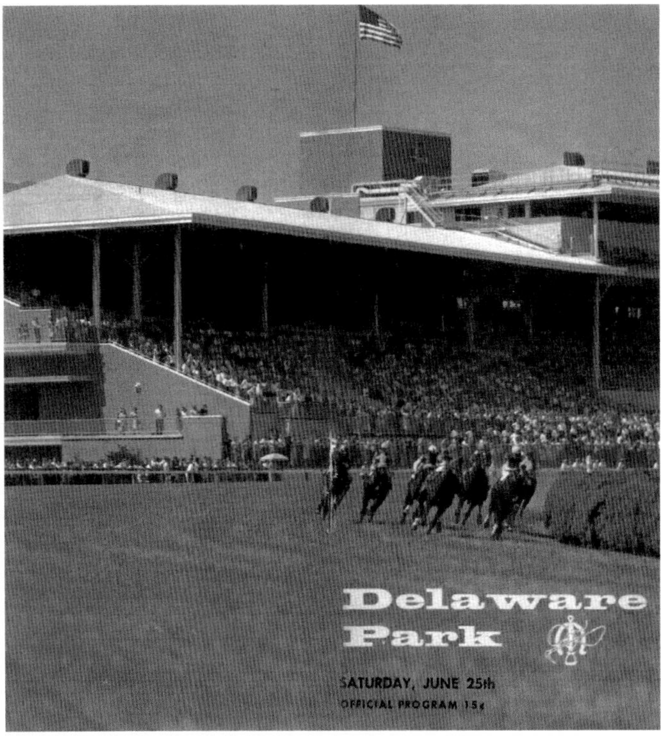

Program, 1954 session.

Delaware Park was always open to innovation. In 1955, the track hosted a balloting contest to determine the best fillies and mares in American history. Designed to draw attention to the Delaware Handicap, New Castle Handicap and the Delaware Oaks, the balloting listed the top forty-five fillies in racing history, including the likes of Firense, Beewitch, Twilight Tear and Galorette, and asked the fans to arrive at the park and take part in the balloting.[91] The DuPont Laboratories also developed a new film-processing technique that could develop final-finish racing movies in forty-eight seconds.

In the 1950s, Delaware Park began to receive direct competition in its local area. Much of the revenue had come from Philadelphia, but three new racetracks had been built in New Jersey, including the Garden State Raceway just across the river. By 1957, Delaware Park would only have seven "open" dates on which no other racing was scheduled in the immediate vicinity of the park. The owners and management were at a loss as to how to attract a new base of revenue to the park, to take some of the steam away from the other racetracks. The new avenue for success would come from not one of the management, but the wisdom of Helen Stairwelt, one of the office staff, who suggested that they hold special races for the fillies. After consideration of the idea, they came up with the Distaff Big Three, a trio of races for fillies consisting of the Oaks, New Castle Handicap and the Delaware Handicap.[92]

By 1957, Delaware Park had fully become what it is today: a family-friendly place devoted more to the love of the horse than the obsession with the bet. It is this attractiveness that still endears Delaware Park to the local community. As it grew,

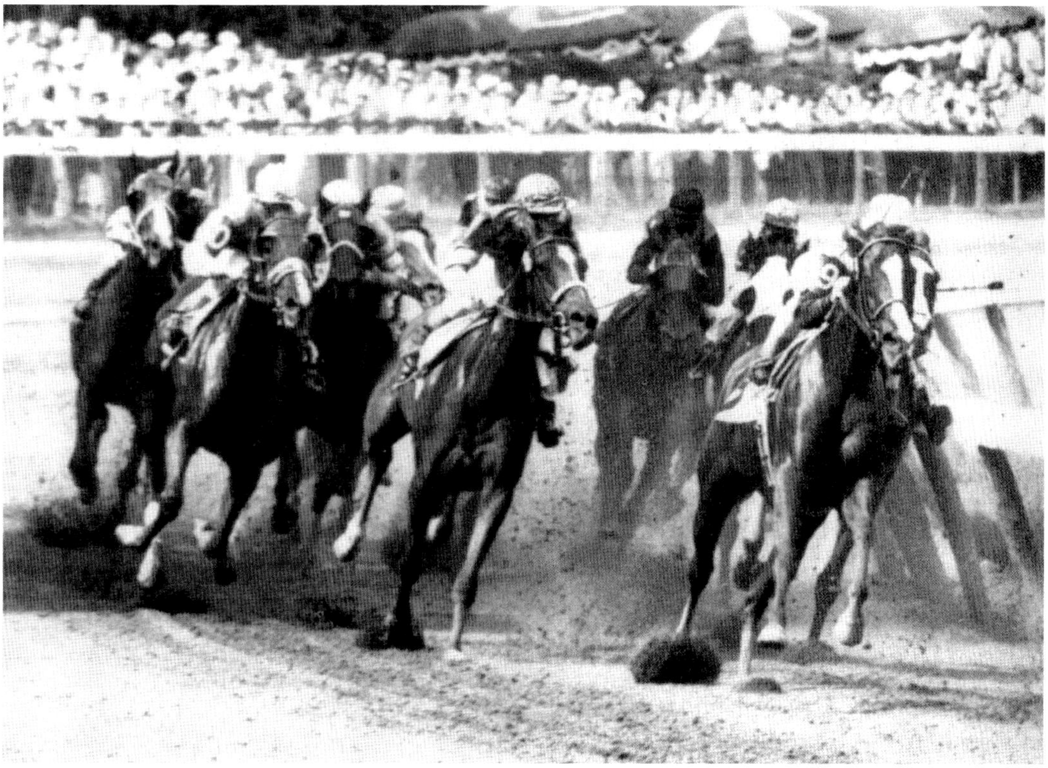

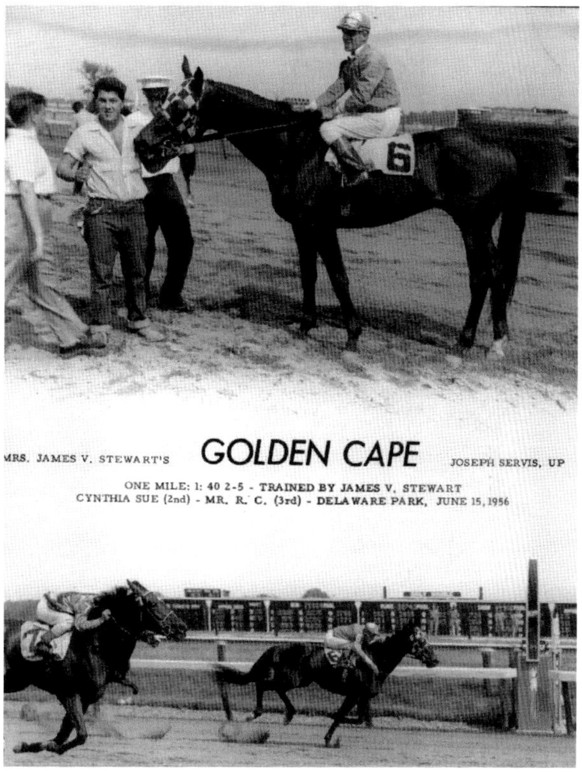

Avove: DuPont's Foxcatcher Farms' Parlo was fifth, three wide, but went on to win the 1955 Delaware Handicap.

Right: Golden Cape, winner on June 15, 1956. James V. Stewart, trainer, Joseph Servis, up.

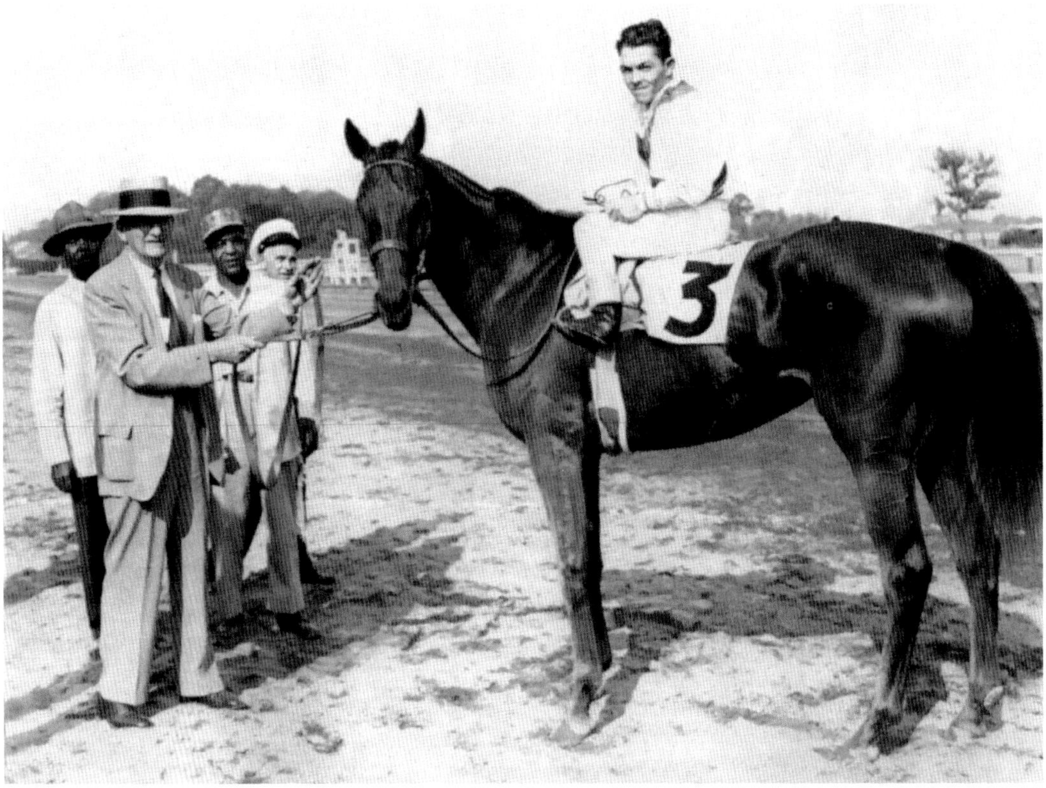

Delaware Handicap.

Delaware Park managed to remain essentially what it was in the beginning, a quiet, country horse park. It operated as a neighbor to the community, turning over its facilities free of charge to such neighborhood organizations as the Wilmington Kennel Club, Knights of Columbus and Jaycees for religious rallies, free government campaigns and safe-driving demonstrations. Sometimes, though, the family-friendly atmosphere led to unforeseen consequences:

> *Last summer a very small child turned up at the office of the security police, detached from his parents. He was stroked and petted and fed ice cream until the loud-speaker affected a family reunion. Every day for an entire racing week, the same kid showed up lost. "Lady," said an attendant at length, "could you please keep an eye on your own boy?" "Could you," she snapped, "please stop giving him ice cream cones?"*[93]

In 1958–59, a $2.8 million expansion was completed, including the building of a new clubhouse and the enlargement of the grandstand, resulting in the doubling of the seating capacity. Televisions were added and the winner's circle was built. During the same time, the Delaware State Legislation approved an increase in the parimutuel "bite" from 10 to 12 percent, with the state and track each getting an additional 1 percent. Donald Ross, in a statement released after the meeting, also said "the [track's] 1937

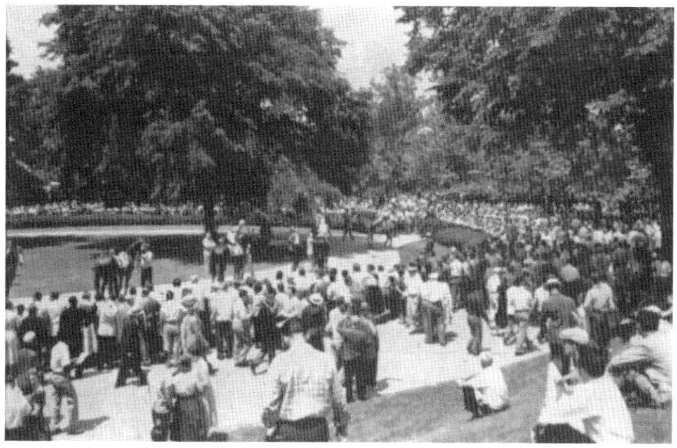

The beautiful paddock in 1957. *Reprinted from the* Saturday Evening Post *magazine, © 1957. Saturday Evening Post Society.*

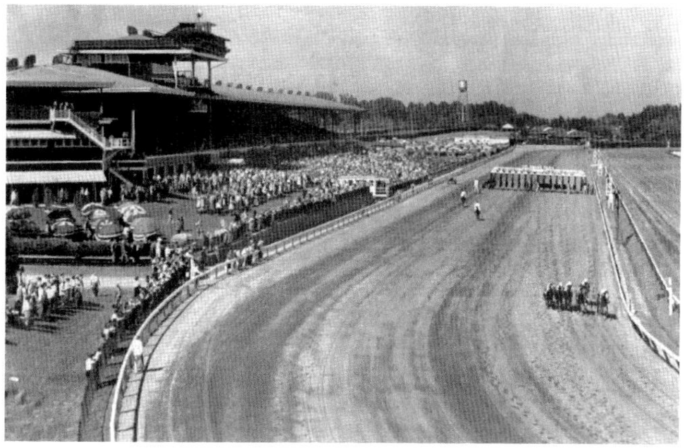

They're off! *Reprinted from the* Saturday Evening Post *magazine, © 1957. Saturday Evening Post Society.*

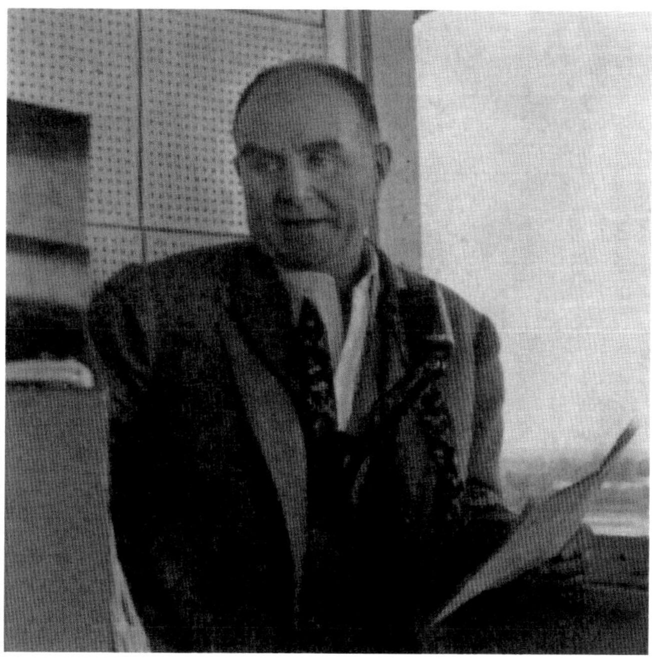

Byran Field in 1957. *Reprinted from the* Saturday Evening Post *magazine, © 1957. Saturday Evening Post Society.*

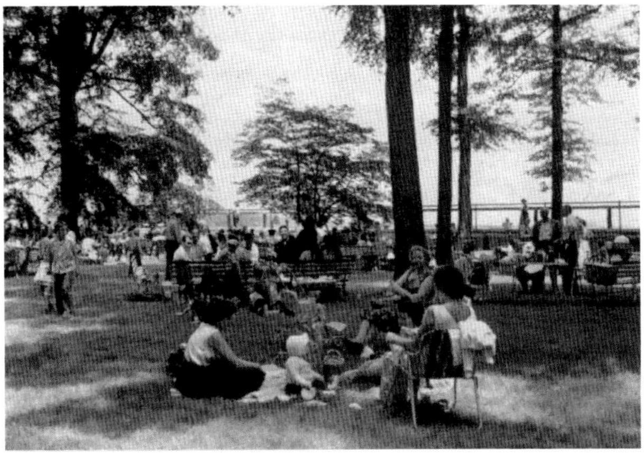

The picnic grounds are fun for the whole family. *Reprinted from the* Saturday Evening Post *magazine, © 1957. Saturday Evening Post Society.*

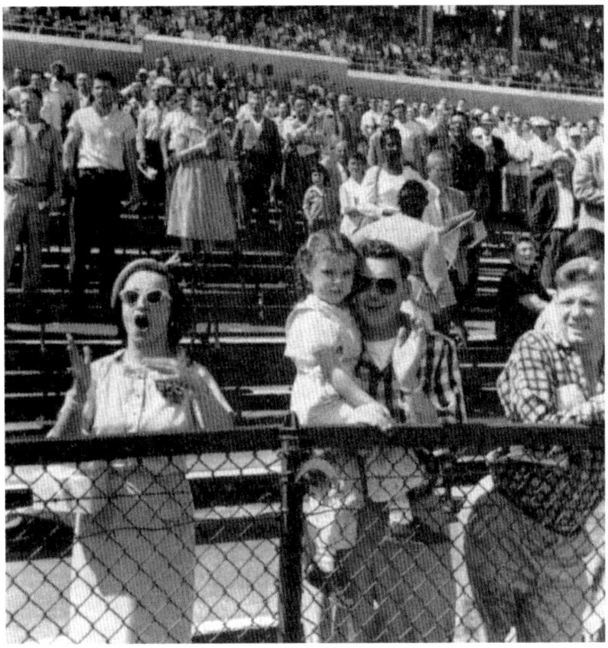

Everyone loves to watch the horses. *Reprinted from the* Saturday Evening Post *magazine, © 1957. Saturday Evening Post Society.*

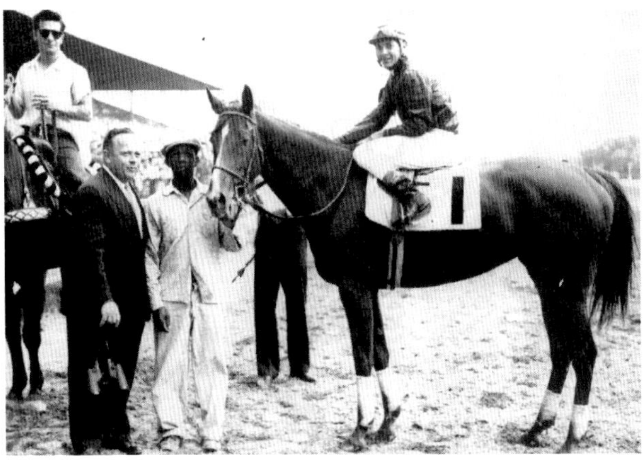

Trainer H.A. Jones and Calumet Farms' Princess Twin, after winning the 1957 Delaware Handicap.

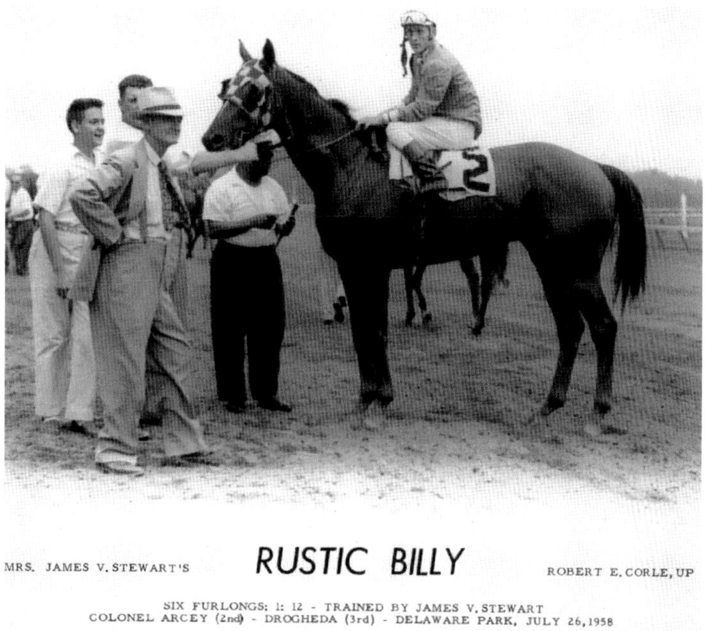

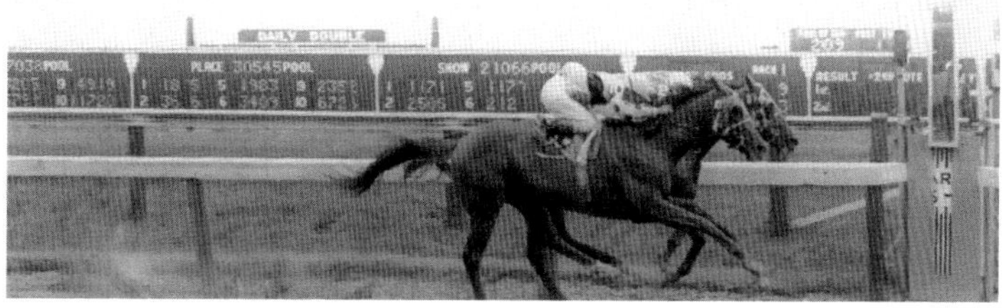

Rustic Billy, winner on July 26, 1958. James Stewart, trainer, Robert E. Corle, up.

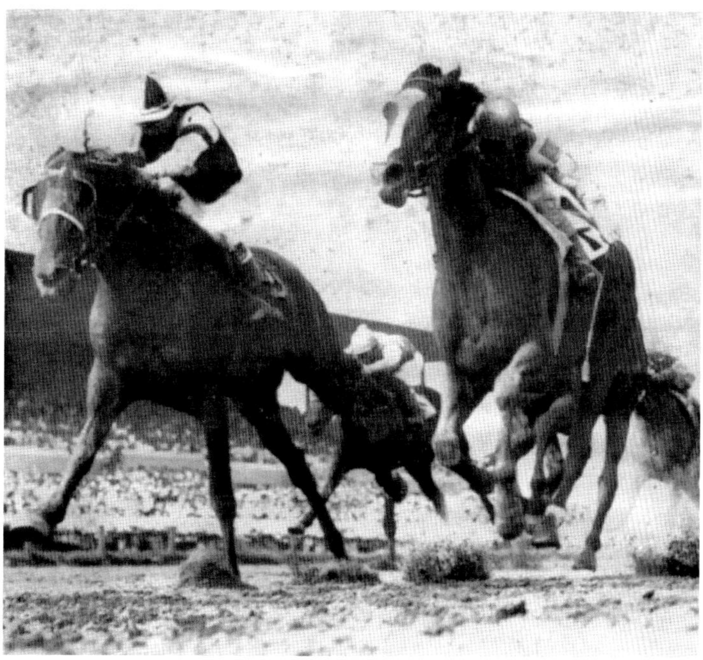

1958 Delaware Handicap.

starting policy of [paying] no dividends to stockholders has been adhered to through twenty years, and no future change is contemplated."[94]

Christiana Stable's trainer, Henry Clark, was a longtime favorite at Delaware Park in the 1950s and 1960s. He trained Endine, who won the 1958 Delaware Handicap. The grandson of famous Maryland horseman and trainer William Jennings Sr., he learned the trade from his grandfather and began his career working for Liz Whitney. Whitney's Blue Cypress was Clark's first stakes winner. He then changed stables to work for Henry and Jane Lunger. He became well known for conditioning fillies and distaffers. He

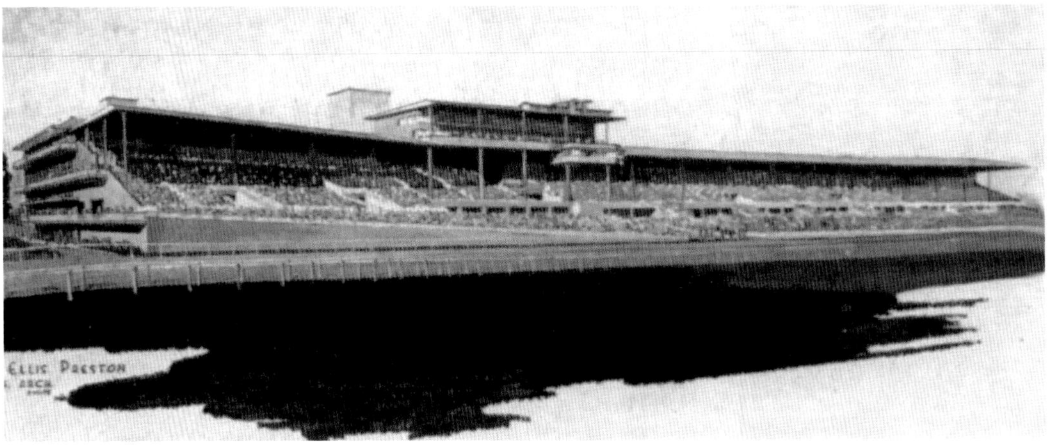

Artist's conception of the remodeling, completed for the 1961 session.

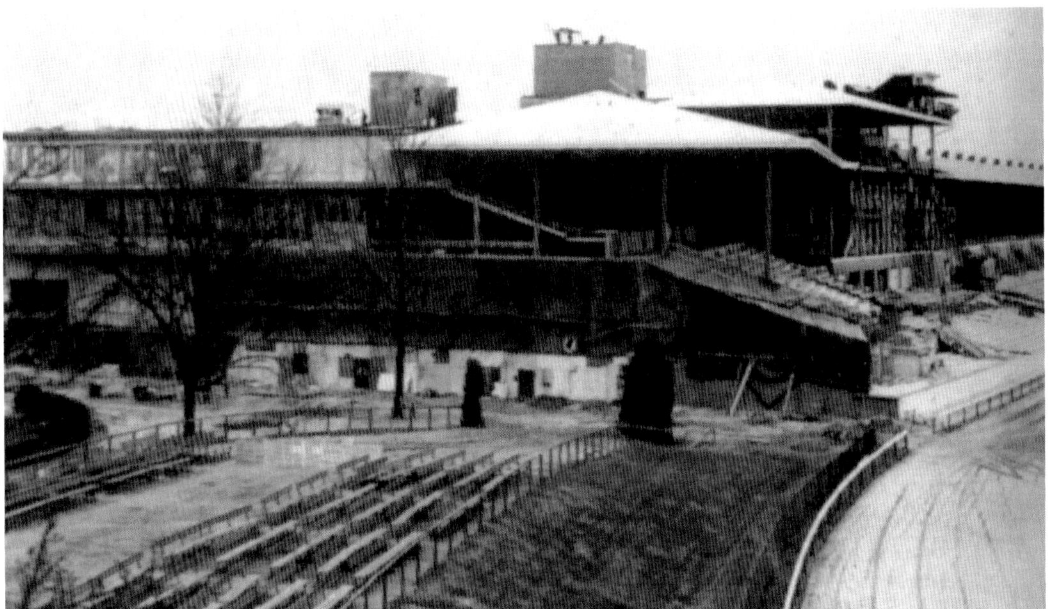

Work on the new clubhouse, 1961.

trained Temped, Obeah and Endine. He was inducted into the National Horseracing Hall of Fame in 1982, and continued working with horses up to his death in 1999 at the age of ninety-nine.[95]

Improvements included a new four-tiered clubhouse, expanded grandstands and parking and a new winner's enclosure.[96] Delaware Park opened its season on May 29, 1959, to a large crowd of 12,665, a record for a weekday opening.[97] The remodeled park got rave reviews. It was reported that the "new clubhouse, all levels connected by escalators, is expected to sell itself to the patrons. The brick and steel structure has a series of galleries with balconies overlooking the paddock. In the grandstand area escalators are also available as is a new air-conditioned cafeteria." Opening day was celebrated as "fraternal civic day," with races honoring the Nur Temple Shriners, Knights of Columbus, B'Nai B'Brith, New Castle County Firemen's Association and the Wilmington Junior Chamber of Commerce. Another opening day highlight was the first of a series of weekly fashion shows in the clubhouse, beginning with one by John Wannamaker.[98]

On July 4, 1959, the famed Japanese horse Hakuchikara was entered into the Sussex Turf Handicap at Delaware Park; he was the first Japanese horse run in America. He had finished far back in the Bowling Green Handicap at Belmont Park, but was the winner at Santa Anita the previous winter.[99] However, at Delaware Park he fared poorly, and failed to even show.

Two long-standing track records were set in two successive weekends, which have stood for forty-six years. On June 18, 1960, Canadian-owned Victoria Park blazed around the track in the Richards Stakes, easily beating Tompion to finish the 1$^{1}/_{8}$-mile

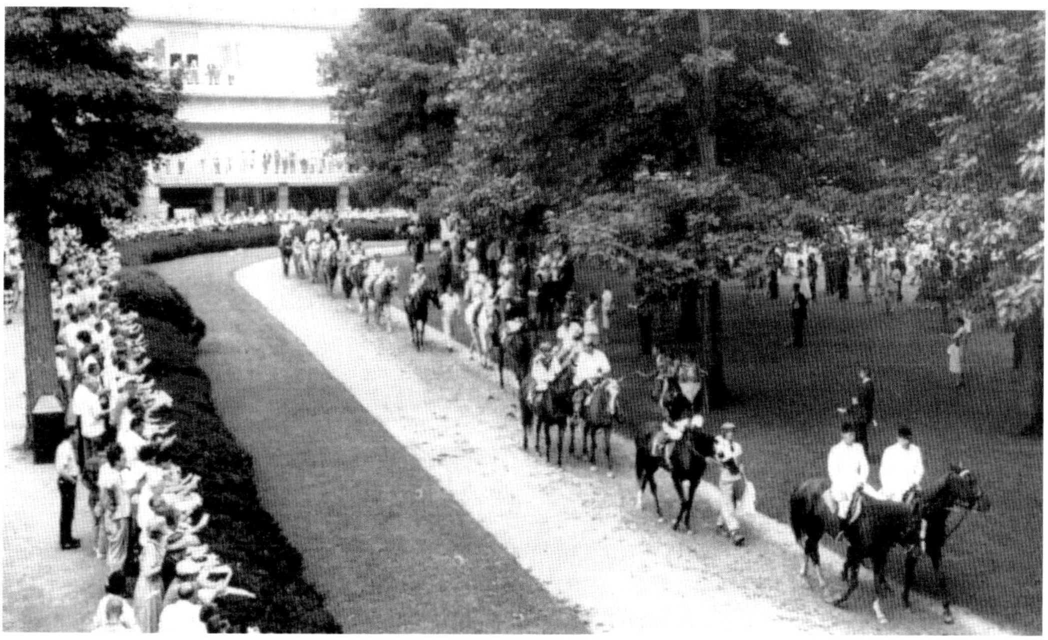

The new paddock.

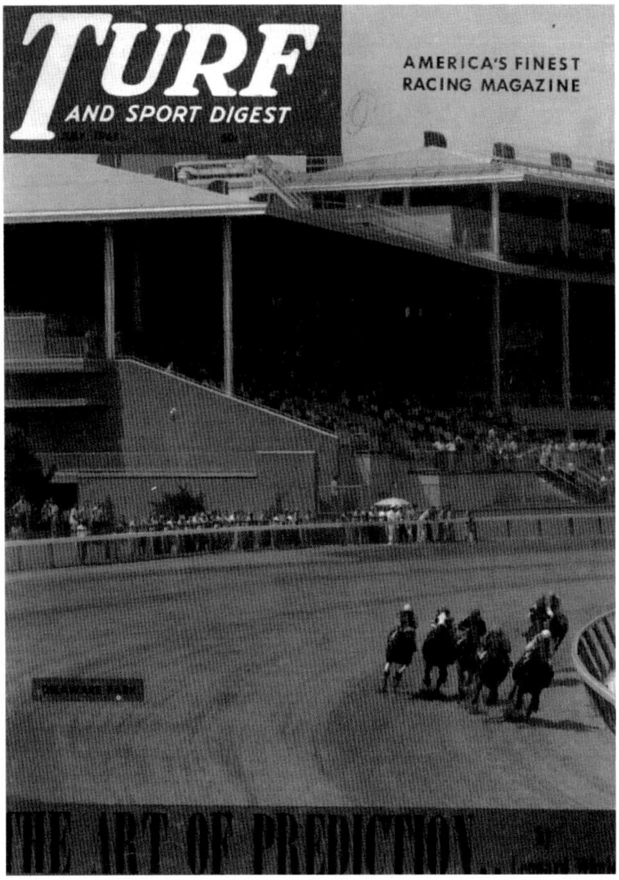

The new Delaware Park was unveiled on the July 1961 cover of *Turf and Sport Digest.* Turf and Sport Magazine, *July 1961.*

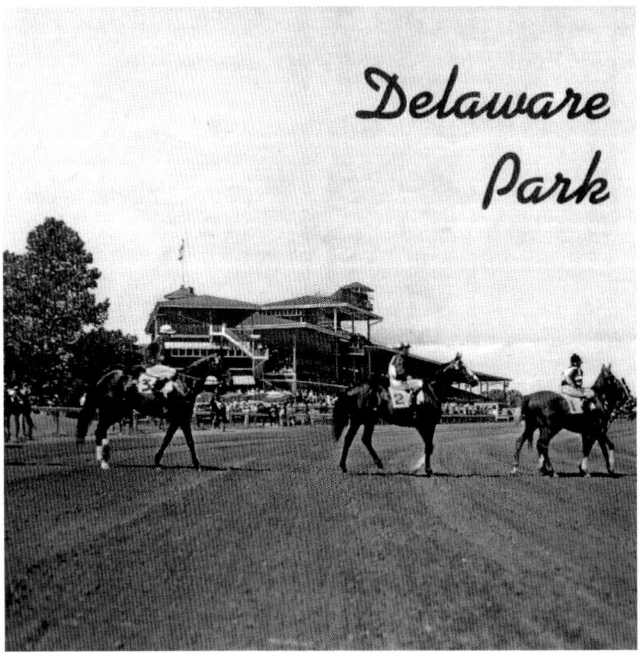

Program, 1960 session.

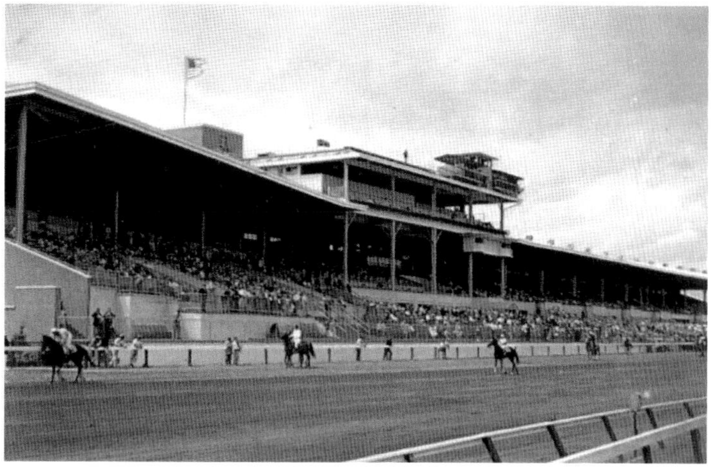

1960s postcard, after the remodeling.

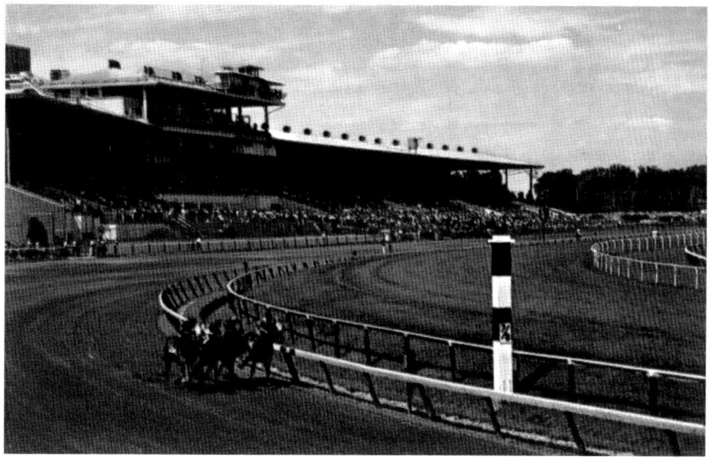

1960s postcard, after the remodeling.

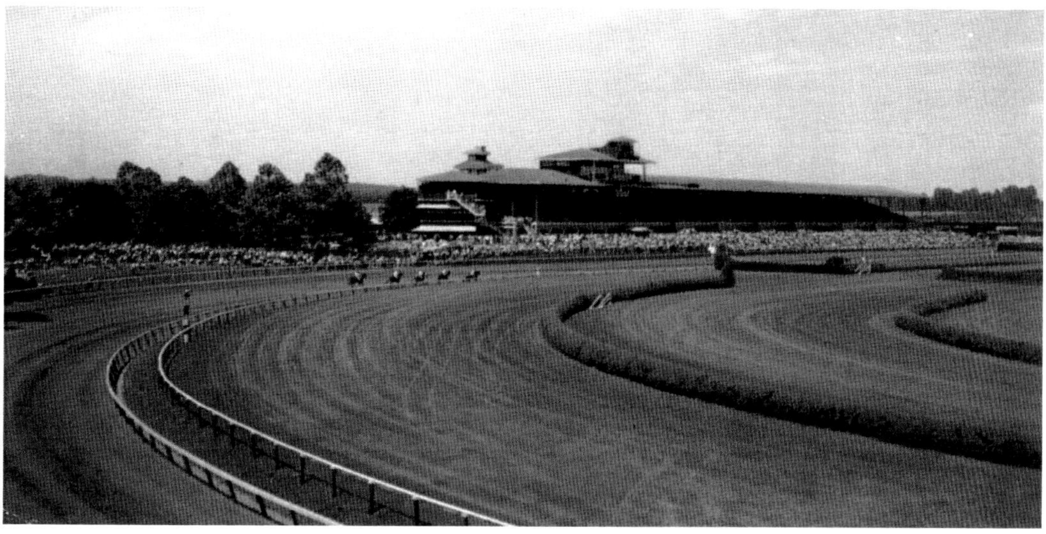

Another view.

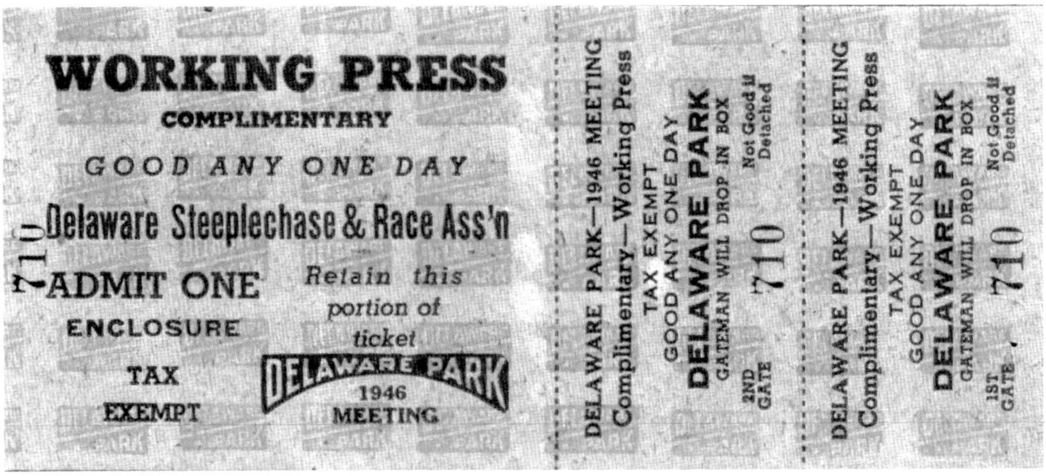

1960s press pass.

race with 1:47.40.[100] In addition, the benefits of the expansion were measurable, for by 1960 the park contributed $3 million in tax revenue to the state.[101]

Fans of the park on June 25, 1960, also witnessed a new record set for the one mile. In the sixth race, the horse Ashlar, by Shoestring Stable, won the $10,000 Busher Handicap. Ashlar reduced the former mark set by Conestoga earlier in the season by four-fifths of a second.[102]

The Story of Kelso

The best horse doesn't always win the race.
–old Irish proverb

However, records notwithstanding, interest in racing in the early 1960s was generated by one amazing horse—Kelso. Kelso (April 4, 1957–October 16, 1983) was considered the fourth best thoroughbred in American racing history, behind Man o' War, Secretariat and Citation.

Kelso's trainer was Nebraska-born Carl Hanford. Carl was one of ten children, three of whom became jockeys in their teenage years. In 1933, Carl Hanford followed his brother Buddy Hanford to New York, and although Buddy died in 1935 in a freak accident at the Pimlico Racetrack in Baltimore, Carl stayed on as a jockey, and won on the first race run at Suffolk Downs, in July 1935.

Carl's brother, Ira "Babe" Hanford, the youngest boy in the family, was also a notable jockey. Ira was on the 20–1 long shot Bold Venture when the horse won the Kentucky Derby on May 2, 1936. The year before, Ira Hanford was honored to meet with Jim Braddock, the heavyweight champion of the world. Ira went on to ride the great Seabiscuit as a three-year-old; Assault, who won the Triple Crown in 1946; and Middleground, who won the Derby and Belmont Stakes in 1950. Ira stopped racing in 1953, and enjoys a lengthy retirement in Ocala, Florida. In 2005, he was honored by the Kentucky Derby Museum as the longest living Kentucky Derby winner, and left his handprint in cement at the Gait House's Gallop to Glory museum.[103]

After serving in the army, Carl Hanford returned to New York and there trained the filly LA Corresora, winner of five stakes races. An opportunity arose in January of 1960 to go to work for Allaire DuPont, who needed a new trainer. Carl got the job and was given responsibility for a feisty gelding named Kelso.

Under Carl Hanford's watchful hand, Kelso proceeded to win eight of nine races as a three-year-old in 1960. Hanford commented, "Kelso was an extremely determined horse. If he saw a horse in front, he wanted to get to him. You could take him back or send him to the front. He was an extremely sound horse who was light on his feet with

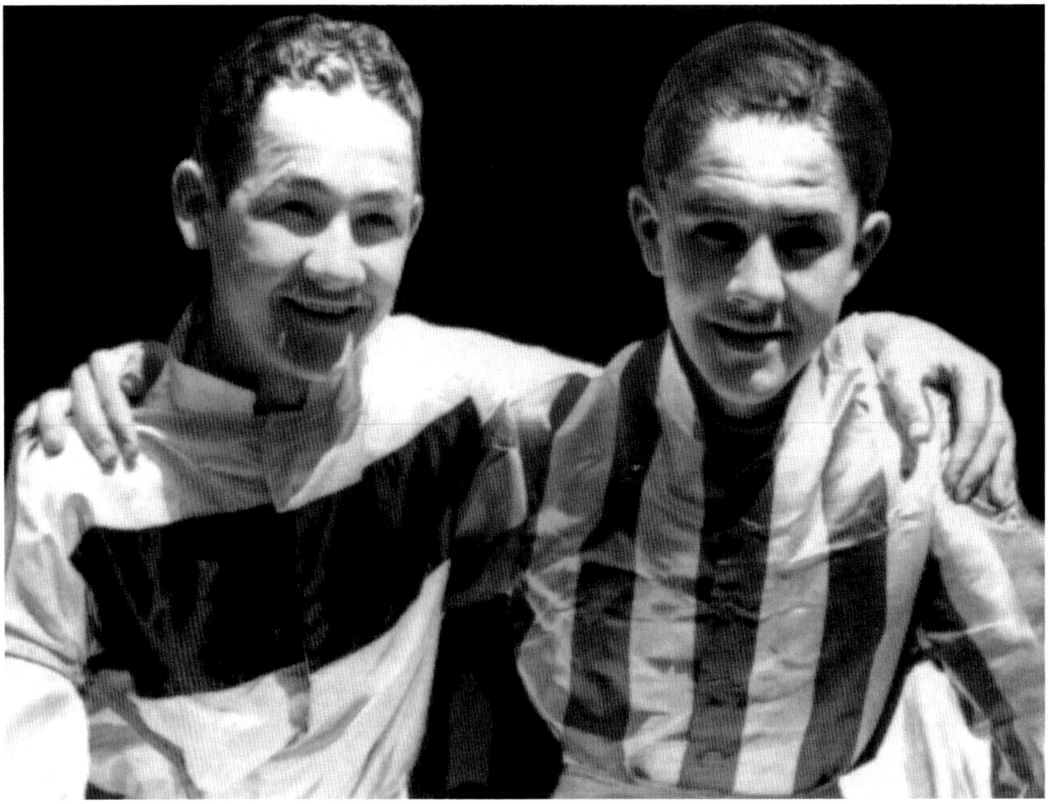

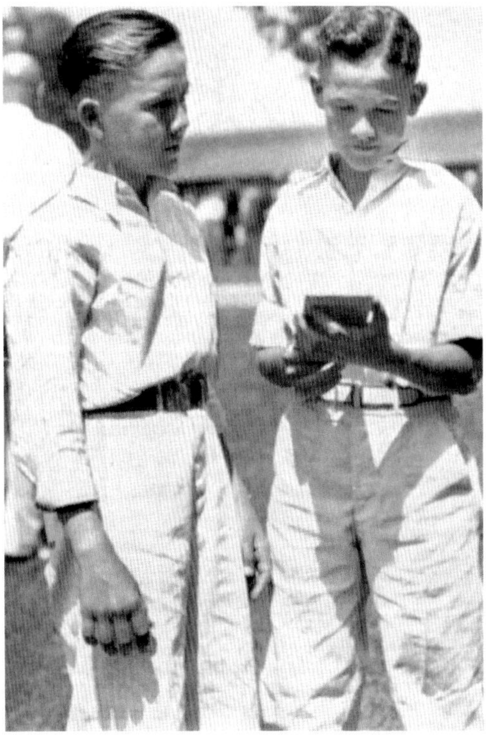

Above: Carl Hanford (left) with brother Ira Hanford at Saratoga in the 1930s.

Left: Carl and Ira Hanford as young boys. Post Time *magazine, 1935.*

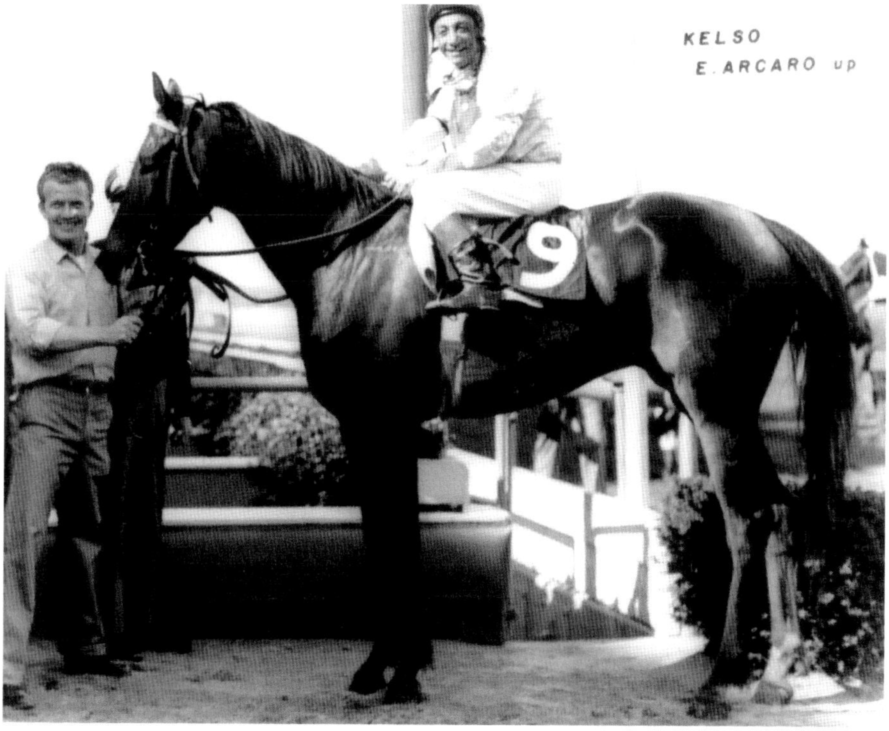

Kelso with Bill Hall. Eddie Arcaro up, circa 1961.

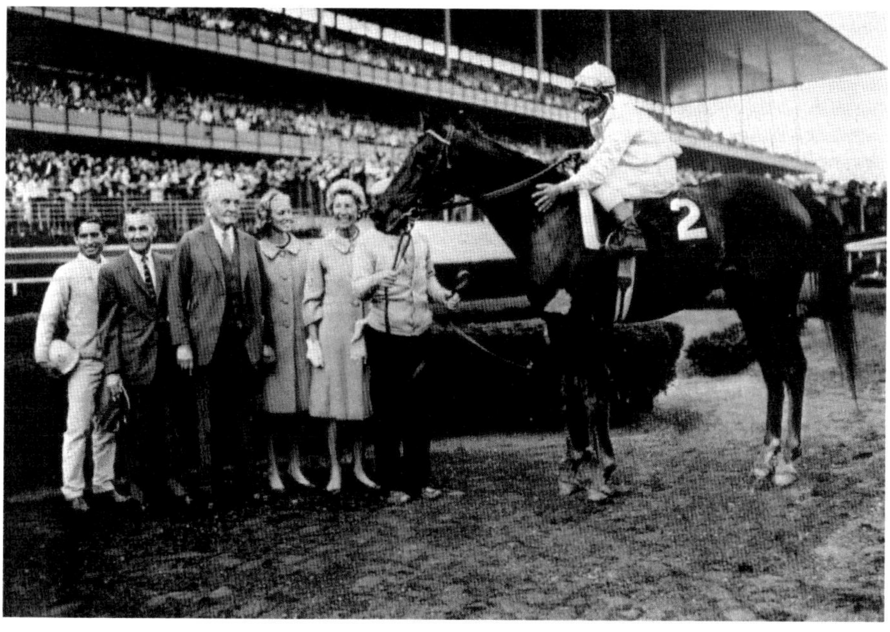

Kelso, in his third victory at the Woodward Stakes, with Dick Jennkin (exerciser), Carl Hanford (trainer), Samuel A. Croser, Miss Lana DuPont and Mrs. Richard C. DuPont (owner), with Ismael "Milo" Valenzuela up. History of Thoroughbred Racing in America, *Robertson, 1965.*

incredible balance. Kelso could wheel on a dime, spinning around in a circle and never letting his feet touch each other."

Hanford would later recount:

> *Kelso was an easy horse to train. He loved to run and hated to see himself get beat. He just didn't want other horses getting past him. When Kelso ran his best races, I don't see how any horse could beat him. I saw Kelso win his first race as a 2-year-old at Atlantic City. I knew he was a pretty good horse after he got running. I started to realize just how good he was when he won the first Jockey Gold Cup as a 3-year-old. He was actually a pretty light horse as a 3-year-old. He got better as a 4-year-old, but didn't really develop until he was a 5-year-old. He just wouldn't have made it to the Derby.*[104]

Kelso went on to be unstoppable, whipping every horse on every track in every field condition, and was named as the only Horse of the Year for five consecutive years, from 1960 to 1964. Kelso was bred by Allaire DuPont and stabled in Chesapeake City, Maryland. He was the grandson of Triple Crown winner Count Fleet, and he won everything from six furlongs to two miles, on grass, in slop six inches thick and often burdened with top weights up to 136 pounds. In almost half of his victories—he had thirty-nine in sixty-three starts—Kelso set or equaled track records. At distance greater than a mile and a half he was probably the greatest horse who ever lived. No horse ever beat him at two miles; he won the Jockey Club Gold Cup at that distance an unthinkable five straight times. Nearing eight years old, in his last big race at the 1964 International, Kelso romped home in 2:23.4 on grass—the fastest any horse had ever run on this continent.[105]

He raced at Delaware Park only once, as an eight-year-old in the 1965 Diamond State Handicap, in which he showed his heels to younger rivals and scored an easy 3¼-length victory in the $21,850 race. The eight-year-old gelding left little doubt that he was in the running for a sixth straight Horse of the Year crown. He finished the 1¹/₁₆-mile in 1:42²/₅, three-fifths of a second slower than the track record. The world's leading money-winning thoroughbred, owned and bred by Mrs. Richard C. DuPont, was ridden by his regular jockey, Ismael Valenzuela, at the top weight of 120 pounds. The victory was worth $14,202 to Kelso's owner and pushed the horse closer to becoming the first $2 million winner. His earnings after the race totaled $1,908,064.

Hobeau Farm's Kilmoray was second to the prohibitive favorite, and had three lengths to spare over Robert F. Robert's Big Brigade; Knightly Manner was a nose back. It was the second start of the year for Kelso, who had finished third in a surprise preparation race a week previous. Only win and place betting were permitted because of the small field. Kelso paid $2.60 and $2.20 for $2. Carl Hanford, his trainer, said, "It was a good race for Kelso. We wanted to get him tight. He ships to New York tomorrow and most likely will go next in the Brooklyn Handicap July 24 at Aqueduct. He's eligible for the Monmouth Handicap next Saturday. However, three consecutive Saturdays may not be to his liking." Jockey Valenzuela added, "He seemed like the Kelso of old. He went right about his business and I had dead aim on the leader all the time."[106]

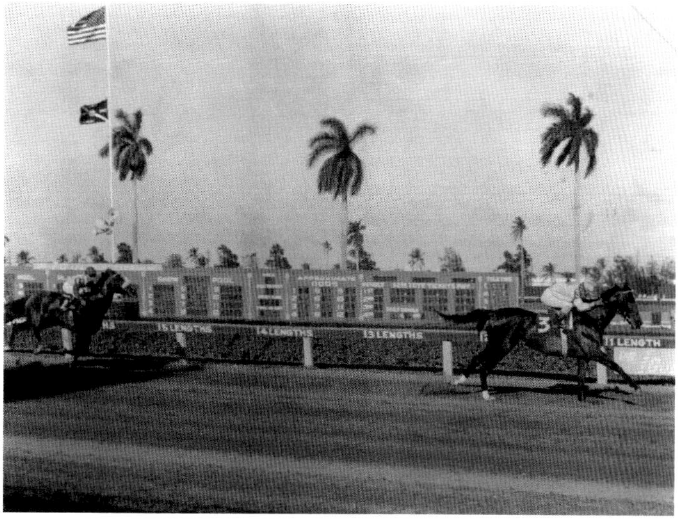

Kelso winning the 1963 Gulfstream Park Handicap, Milo Valenzuela up.

This was the one and only time that Kelso raced at Delaware Park. He only ran four more races in 1965, winning at the Whitney Stakes at Saratoga and the Stymie Handicap at the Aqueduct, and placing at the Brooklyn Handicap. The following year, the nine-year-old raced his last on March 2, 1966, in the Purse at Hialeah Park. Kelso ended his racing career as the all-time leading money earner, with $1,997,896. After that he was retired to Mrs. DuPont's Woodstock Farm in Chesapeake City, Maryland, where he shared his stall with several companion dogs. He even had his own mailbox there to handle all the fan mail he received.

Mrs. DuPont turned Kelso into a fox hunter and rode him on fox hunts until 1974, when his arthritis became so bad that he became just a pensioner. Mrs. DuPont told Jim Bolus, "Kelso was as gentle as could be. He could jump over big fences. He went on like he'd done it all his life."

On October 15, 1983, for the running of the Jockey Club Gold Cup and Champagne Stakes, Kelso was transported to Belmont Park for a special appearance with Forego as part of a benefit for the Thoroughbred Retirement Foundation. Kelso was accompanied on the trip from Maryland by his companion for over fifteen years, a gelding called Pete (who raced as Sea Spirit and won the New Jersey Futurity in 1961). Kelso was twenty-six at the time and many said he looked as good as Forego, who was thirteen years younger. A crowd of 32,493 at Belmont Park that afternoon gave the two a thunderous ovation as they appeared together for the first and only time. The day after the Belmont appearance Kelso and Pete were brought back to Maryland, and shortly after arriving at the farm, Kelso died suddenly. The press speculated that the trip may have been too much for him. The cause of death was believed to have been colic. Kelso was buried at the farm.[107] Joe Hirsch, writer for the *Daily Forum*, wrote: "Once upon a time there was a horse named Kelso. But only once."[108]

But the story of Hanford and Delaware Park doesn't stop there, for his daughter, Gail Hanford, grew up around the park and eventually decided to carry on her father's

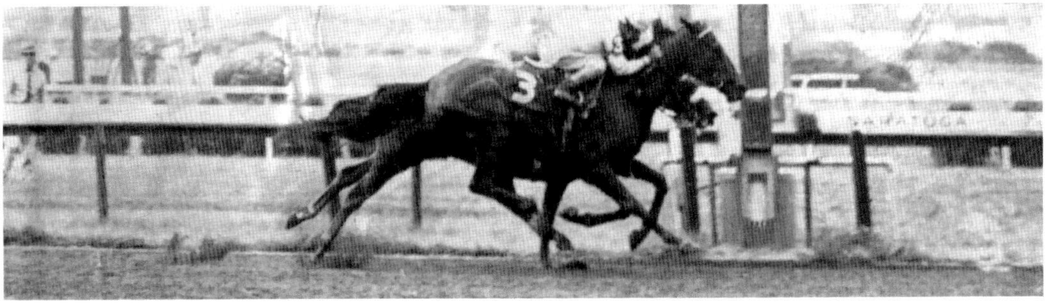

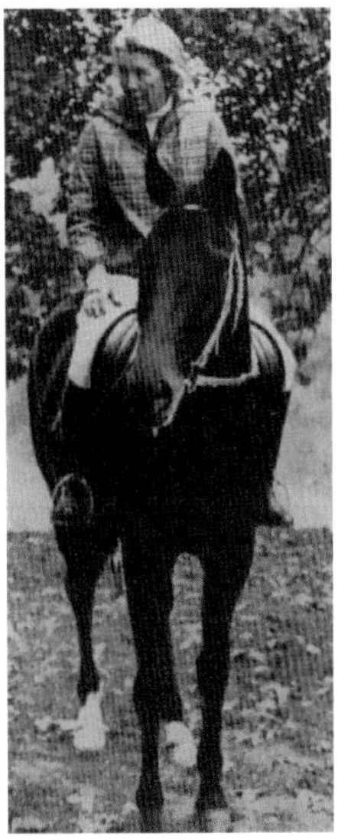

Above: Kelso, beating Malicious by a nose in the Whitney at Saratoga in 1966.

Left: Mrs. Richard C. DuPont, owner of Kelso and Bohemia Stables. Turf and Sport Magazine, *August 1967.*

legacy. Now a successful trainer in her own right, as of 1993 Gail Hanford "had three clients, the Rooney brothers. A family connection between the Hanfords and the Rooneys—Carl Hanford trained horses for the Rooneys' father—created the current owner-trainer relationship."

One of the brothers, Dan Rooney, owner of the Pittsburgh Steelers football team, placed a six-year-old from Ireland named Marabeau Special with Ms. Hanford. "She's really done a good job," he said. "Before Gail got the horse, it was not doing so great." Since she began training Marabeau Special, the horse had won three races, finished third once and fourth once. All that in just six races.

Gail Hanford explained her motivation in an interview: "Working seven days, starting around 6:30 a.m. and ending around noon, only to go back for feeding time around 4:30 p.m. for a few more hours," she is completely responsible for the care of her owners' horses, from feeding to bathing, exercising and grooming. She also picks the races in which the horses run. In the end, she explained her passion for the ponies this way: "You kind of have to be in love with animals to work with them every day. The owners are in it for the love of the sport, but the people who put in 24-hour days...why else are they doing it but for the love of the animals?"[109]

An Afternoon with Carl Hanford

As part of this book, the author had the great honor of spending an afternoon with Hall of Fame trainer Carl Hanford on February 16, 2008. Below is a transcript of the interview.

Interviewer: This is Hall of Fame trainer Carl Hanford. You were born in Nebraska?
Hanford: Yes, in Freebury, Nebraska.
Interviewer: And you come from a large family?
Hanford: Yes, ten children in the family. My dad and one of my brothers suffocated in a fire when I wasn't even two years old at the time. My younger brother wasn't even born at the time. And then we moved to Omaha, Nebraska, and my mother remarried another man.
Interviewer: I know you and Buddy and Ira were all jockeys. How did you get involved in becoming a jockey?
Hanford: Well, we didn't live too far from the AkSarBen racetrack in Omaha, and the race owners got my older brother Buddy interested in riding horses in the AkSarBen racetrack in Omaha, and he left home and became a rider. He was a real good one, and my brother Ira was a good rider, too. I wasn't that good.
Interviewer: I expect you were too.
Hanford: Well, I wasn't as good as either one of them. Ira won the Derby in 1936.
Interviewer: I read on the computer that he recently was celebrated as the oldest living Kentucky Derby rider.
Hanford: Yeah, right. We were down in Kentucky for that. A year later I was in the Hall of Fame.
Interviewer: How long did you ride as a jockey?
Hanford: About five years. And I started training horses about the time the army got me.
Interviewer: Where did you serve?
Hanford: I took my basic training in Richmond, Virginia. And I was supposed to go to Reno, Nevada, at the Fremont Station there, and it was stalled and I wound up going to Fort Robinson, Nebraska. And my brother joined the army out there in Nebraska, Ira did. We spent all our army time in Fort Robinson.

Interviewer: So you never had to go overseas?
Hanford: Oh no, we broke horses and mules for the army.
Interviewer: So you became a trainer, then served in the army and then came back as a trainer afterward?
Hanford: I got out of the army and then asked a man I used to ride for, J.U. Graff, who was originally from Canada, but then he wound up with a home and a farm up near Monmouth [New Jersey], and I asked him about a job training horses. And he did! I had one client from Lima, Ohio, J.U. Graff; I bought two horses for him in Hialeah in a dispersal sale. One of them was Jupiter Light, and the other was a horse called Whiffletree. Jupiter Light, I forget who I bought her from, but she was a maiden, they were both maidens, three-year-olds, at the time. Jupiter Light won five of her first six races at Monmouth Park in 1945; that was the first year at Monmouth Park. She was a nice filly. So then I had a stable of horses, I had a public stable and I was a trainer ever since then, after I got out of the army in 1945.
Interviewer: How did you end up down here?
Hanford: Well, I lived in a trailer here, on the other side leading into the park, right at the Delaware Park entrance. I had horses for Art Rooney at different times. I didn't have anything from Mrs. DuPont, but later I got her horses when other trainers quit the job.
Interviewer: Kelso, you started training him in 1960?
Hanford: I had him in the winter, he was at the farm at the time. Not at the farm she has now; she died a few years ago. After I got her horses she was at the other farm, which wasn't big enough for her. This farm was just outside of Middletown, Delaware, right next to Bayard Sharp. We used Bayard Sharp's farm to train when I started training Kelso.
Interviewer: He won his first race in 1960?
Hanford: No, he won his first race in 1959, as a two-year-old. Not that we had him at that time, he ran two races as a two-year-old. The first time I ran him was the next year, in 1960. The first time I ran him we won by ten. [Bill] Hartack rode him.
Interviewer: That's the same Rooney family your daughter trains for now?
Hanford: Right, Art Rooney died about eight or ten years ago, his son owns the horse my daughter trains. He has Yonkers Raceway, he's the president up there. Hartack run him the first two or three times I had time, and Hartack decided to ride a horse in Jamaica, New York, and I told his agent that if I couldn't get Hartack, I would call another rider. So, I called [Eddie] Arcano's agent, and that was the biggest mistake Hartack ever made. Of course, he was Horse of the Year for the next five years.
Interviewer: How was Eddie Arcaro to work with?
Hanford: He was a great rider, but he had some health problems or he would have ridden Kelso his whole life. After he quit, Milo Valenzuela took up riding Kelso.
Interviewer: What are your impressions of Delaware Park, compared to some of the other parks you've been at?
Hanford: Delaware Park is very good. That $100,000 Philly America race is one of the great races in America today, and I think it should be a number one race. The winner of that race goes on to the Breeder's Cup. I was a steward at Delaware Park after I got done training for years.

Interviewer: What does a steward do?
Hanford: He officiates the races. When a horse is disqualified, that's the steward's decision.
Interviewer: Ah, so you were sort of the referee?
Hanford: Yeah, right.
Interviewer: When did you actually retire?
Hanford: When my daughter started training horses, because I didn't want any conflict of interest.
Interviewer: What's your favorite memory of your career?
Hanford: Well, getting Kelso. Of course, I didn't know at the time that Kelso was the Horse of the Year, because he developed gradually. I got the horse from Doc Lee; if he had him he'd have never quit that job. Kelso was Kelso.
Interviewer: He never won the Triple Crown.
Hanford: To begin with, he didn't weigh much over eight hundred pounds. And the time I got him we would have rushed him too much to try to enter the Kentucky Derby. I never thought he was that kind of horse, but I knew he was a pretty nice horse. I took him over as a three-year-old, but I hardly knew anything about him, but that he was a runner. But not that he was Kelso. He won most of his races, he either won them or was right there.
Interviewer: How many does your daughter train?
Hanford: She trains three horses owned by Rooney, and we have two of our own and one by Timmy Rooney. So she has six she trains.
Interviewer: What are the names of the horses you own?
Hanford: Pleasant, and Raleigh. Two of them won five races last year.
Interviewer: Do you get the chance to go over to the park?
Hanford: I go over when my daughter is running her horses, but sometimes I go to Maryland or Philadelphia Park to watch them, but I can see more on the TV.
Interviewer: What's your attitude about the use of slots to keep the horse racing industry going?
Hanford: Well, I think it's really saved Delaware Park. I don't think it would be good for a place like Saratoga. I don't know at the Aqueduct, it would be a good thing. I think it would hurt it at Saratoga, like at Kentucky, I don't think you'll ever see slots at the Derby.
Interviewer: I know your brother had the chance to meet Jim Braddock. Did you get to meet famous people during your career?
Hanford: Well, some. Bayard Sharp was a very nice man, and all the Rooneys are the greatest. Bayard Sharp was a noted man around here; he passed away about two years ago. One thing about being a trainer, if you run in some nice races, you always meet some well-known people.
Interviewer: What was your favorite park of all the places you visited?
Hanford: Saratoga. I don't know, it's just a nice atmosphere up there. The horses do good up there, the horses seem to like the climate up there. Delaware Park is pretty nice too, I like Delaware Park.
Interviewer: Ok, well, any parting thoughts on horse racing?
Hanford: Well, it's a different thing than when I was training horses, it's an altogether different game. I think it's a little bit worse, and I think I'm glad that Kelso was a gelding because he got to run several years. Most of these horses now, the breeding is the big

thing right now, if the horse has any background at all and if he is a good two- or three-year old at all, that's about as far as they go before they go into the breeding shed. I think Kelso would have been the same deal, he would have been in the breeding shed as a four-year-old. But I don't think he would have been an entire horse he would have been Kelso.

Interviewer: Well, thank you, it's certainly an honor to talk with someone with so much history in the industry. Thank you for your time.

The Park During the 1960s and 1970s

The horses paw and prance and neigh,
Fillies and colts like kittens play,
And dance and toss their rippled manes
Shining and soft as silken skeins.
—Oliver Wendell Holmes

Soon after the park was modernized, an unexpected demographic shift began in the surrounding community. The 1960s saw the phenomenon of suburbanization, when concerns about crime and congestion led to the construction of large single-family housing communities. Moderately affluent middle-class families left the inner cities by droves to purchase these homes and establish a different life in the suburbs. Suburban development south of Newark began in the 1950s with the construction of Brookside Park, but it was followed throughout the 1960s by the construction of Rutherford, Chestnut Hill Estates, Todd Estates, Harmony Hills, Sherwood Forest and others, with their pastoral names evoking images of open, safe, green communities. Thousands of homes were built in the area over a ten-year period, forever eliminating the rural nature around the park.

Also of great importance to the shaping of the area was the construction of Interstate 95 at that time. The main north-south corridor on the east coast, I-95 was completed in Delaware in 1963 and was dedicated by President Kennedy. After his assassination later that year, the eleven-mile stretch of the highway that runs through Delaware was renamed the John F. Kennedy Memorial Highway. One of the interchanges on I-95, at Churchmans's Road (Delaware Route 58), provided easy access to either entrance to Delaware Park, allowing the more auto-centric, suburban horse fans rapid access to the park.

Concurrently, the suburbanization of the area also resulted in the construction and operation of a new genre of businesses. Small shopping centers were constructed in the area, providing vital services to the suburban communities. The little crossroads of Ogletown, a few miles from the park, saw the opening of an A&P Grocery store, Mitchell's 5 and 10, a barbershop, liquor store and several restaurants during the

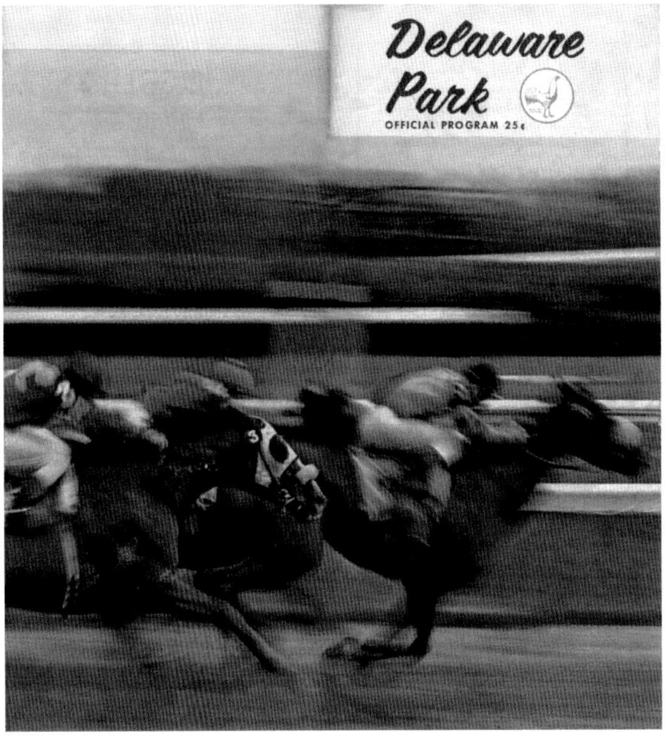

Program, 1966 session.

1960s. These were soon followed by the 1970s construction of the University Plaza Shopping Mall, huge in its day by comparison, and later in the 1980s completion of the Christiana Mall, offering dozens of vendors under one roof.

One notable horse at that time was Mongo. Bred by Mrs. Marion DuPont Scott, Mongo in Scott's Montpellier silks was another local favorite, and a champion as well. Mongo was the American Turf Champion Horse for 1962. He was rated the champion Grass Male by the American Thoroughbred Association in 1963. At the Diamond State Handicap on June 28, 1964, which was run as a betless race, Mongo came out of the gate first, but jockey Wayne Chambers settled him in second place behind Bold Commander. As the horses moved around the stretch turn, Mongo turned on the steam and left Bold Commander in the dust. Bold Commander was a length and a half behind the lead horse.[110] Mongo won the race at 1:43 $^{4}/_{5}$, and netted a purse of $14,430.[111]

On February 15, 1969, President Baird C. Brittingham announced a $4 million modernization plan for the park. The track was intact while the grandstand and clubhouse were improved, and the park opened for a sixty-day program on May 30, concluding on August 9 of that year.[112]

This $4 million renovation was designed to convert the clubhouse into an ultramodern, air-conditioned facility with a tiered trackside dining terrace, luxuriously appointed lounges equipped with closed circuit television and easily accessible, expanded parimutuel wagering area. The entire clubhouse was to be glass enclosed, to

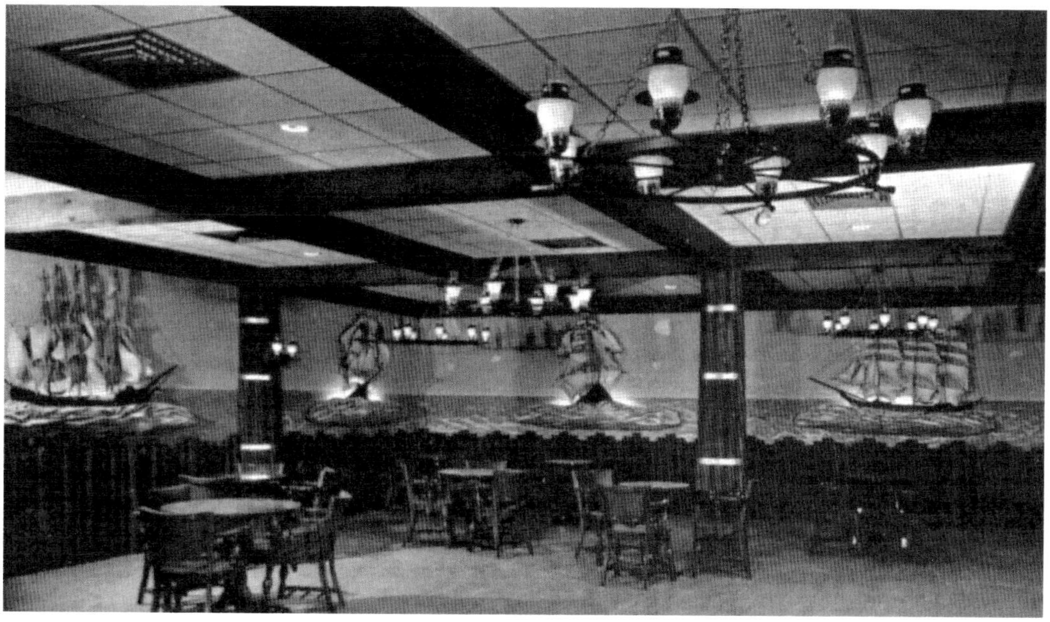

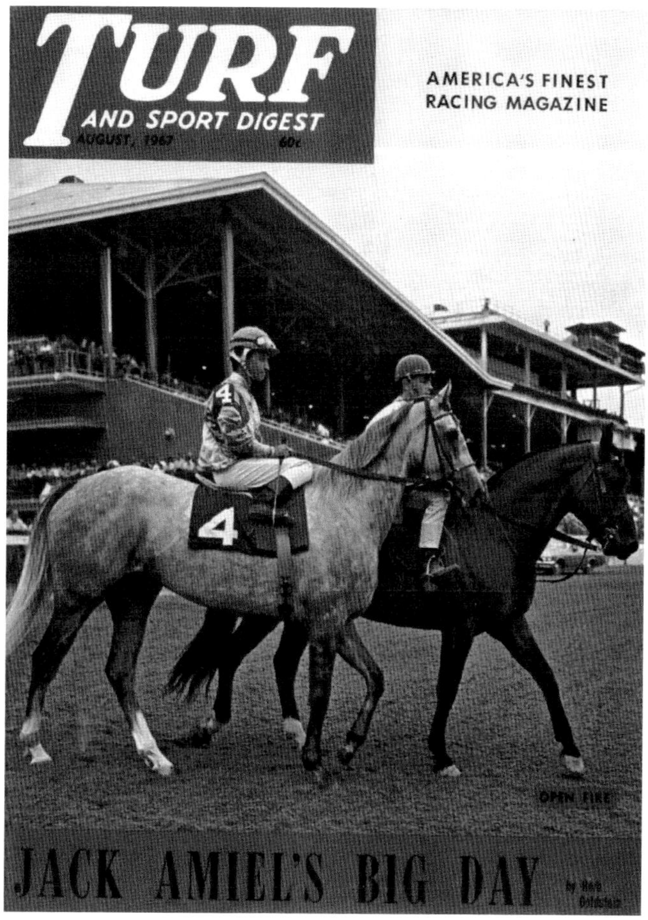

Above: Open Fire at Delaware Park appears in the August 1967 issue of *Turf and Sport Magazine.* Turf and Sport Magazine, *August 1967.*

Right: Sandhill Flight (number eight) battles to a win in the 1967 Tom Roby Chase. Turf and Sport Magazine, *August 1967.*

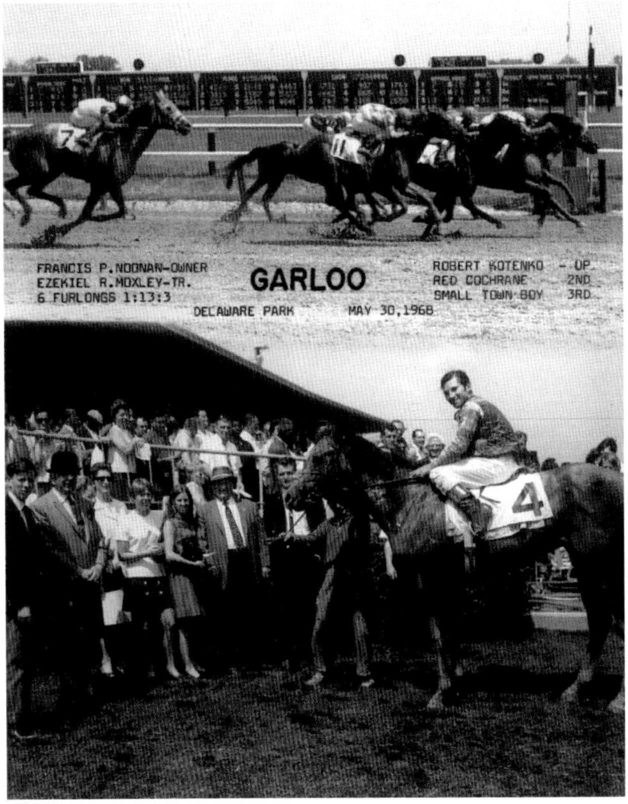

Garloo, winning on May 30, 1968. Francis P. Nodnan, owner, Robert Kotenko, up.

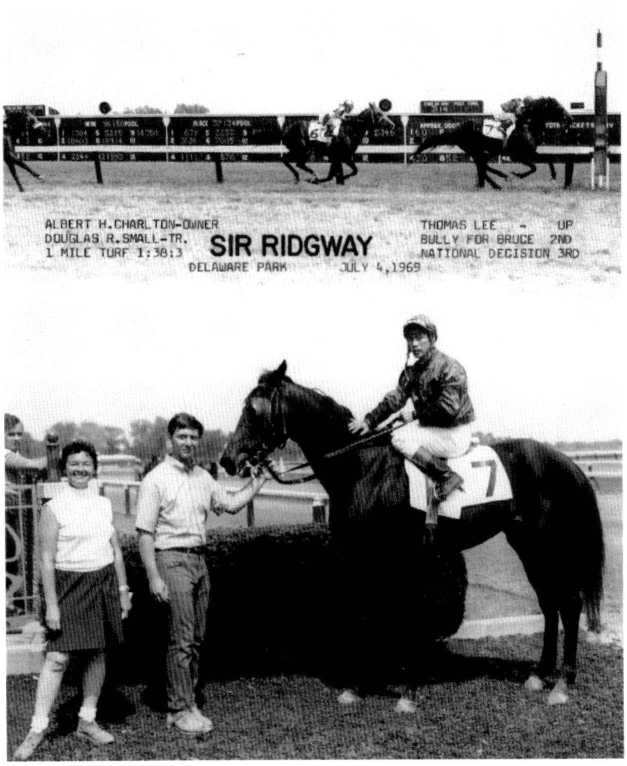

Sir Ridgway, winning on July 4, 1969. Albert H. Charlton, owner, Douglas R. Small, trainer, Thomas Lee, up.

permit temperature control and to provide protection from the elements. However, the "lawn" in front of the main clubhouse would be retained.

Included in the plans submitted by architects and approved by the track's directors were new jockey quarters and a rooftop press box flanked by enclosed working areas for stewards, placing judges, television and radio broadcasters and the film patrol. Also designed were new facilities for the racing department and administrative staff. The offices in use at that time, which had been in use since the track's opening in 1937, would be razed. The work was scheduled to be completed by Memorial Day 1970.[113] When they were completed, the improvements only cost $2.5 million, and "race goers and horsemen alike found more space, facilities, conveniences and beautification at the 700-acre plant."[114]

Another part of the DuPont family gained prominence during the 1960s. Harry and Jane DuPont Lunger had established Christiana Stables in 1937, at the same time that William DuPont was getting Delaware Park operational. This farm has had a long and impressive legacy in the annals of horse racing history in this area. The couple's first winner was Miss Ferdinand, at the 1939 Matron Stakes in New York. Soon afterward was Sea Snack, a stakes winner for three consecutive seasons. Under the Lungers' ownership, Christiana Stables produced forty-five stakes winners. Harry Lunger died in 1976, but Jane Lunger operated the farm until her death in 2001.

Their best-known horse was Go for Wand. This horse won an Eclipse Award in 1989 as the best two-year-old filly after her win at the Breeders Cup. In 1990 she won six stakes races before a catastrophic injury in the Breeders' Cup Distaff, and was buried in the Saratoga infield. After the horse's death, Mrs. Lunger commented,

> *I selected Saratoga. She won two of her biggest stakes there. And Mr. Lunger and I started our racing stable there. It was hard to go back to Saratoga, but it was the right thing to do. Yes, it was like a death in the family. But I've coped with it. I must have received 300 letters from people everywhere, and I answered all of them. She was truly a people horse. She loved racing. She loved to work, to eat, she loved her stable people. Her whole life was joy.*[115]

Other noteworthy horses raised at Christiana Stables were Obeah, Thinking Cap, Endine, Dance Spell, Stem the Tide, Broom Dance and Linkage. Trainers at the stable were Samuel Birch, Jack Healey, Henry Clark, Jim Maloney, Bill Badgett and Jimmy Murphy.[116]

Also gaining prominence was racing legend William Lee "Willie" Shoemaker. He was born on August 19, 1931, in Fabens, Texas, and began to race on March 19, 1949. He won an astounding 8,833 career victories, including 11 Triple Crown races throughout his career. He was on top of Damascus at the Preakness in 1967, Avatar at Belmont in 1975 and Ferdinand at the Kentucky Derby in 1986. He was inducted into the National Museum of Racing Hall of Fame in 1958, won the Eclipse Award for Outstanding Jockey in 1981 and was inducted into the Delaware Park Hall of Fame in 2007. Willie Shoemaker died on October 12, 2003.[117]

Local sporting fans were thrilled with the addition of the new Dover Downs to the state's attractions, in 1968. This dual-purpose facility was designed to accommodate

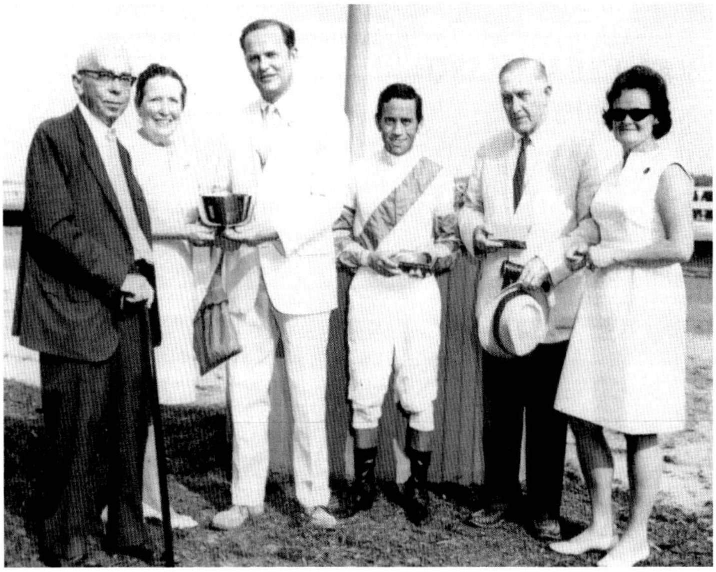

Christiana Stables' Harry W. Lunger, Mrs. Lunger, then-Governor Russell W. Peterson, jockey John L. Rotz, trainer Henry Clark and Mrs. Peterson, after Obeah's first win in 1969.

two sports: horse racing and motorsports. The first motor race there was the NASCAR Winston Cup Race, also known as the Mason-Dixon 500, won in its inaugural year by the famed Richard Petty. During the first two years, a thoroughbred meet was followed by a harness meet. The first harness race was held there on November 19, 1969. Thoroughbred racing was eventually dropped to benefit Delaware Park, but the venue has since grown to be a major site for harness racing on the East Coast.

In 1971, the state legislature changed the laws to permit Sunday gaming. "Sunday racing made its debut in Delaware today. More than 8,000 fans turned out at Dover Downs and wagered a record $573,856 through the pari-mutuel machines...Following the lead of Delaware Park, which announced it would begin Sunday racing when its season opened in May, Dover Downs added Sunday racing to its regular schedule."[118]

The general public was again attracted to thoroughbred horse racing in 1973, with the amazing victories by Secretariat. Born on March 30, 1970, he won the 1973 Triple Crown; he was the first horse to accomplish that feat in twenty-five years. His win at Belmont was by an astounding thirty-one lengths, one of the widest margins in horse racing history. In a career that spanned only sixteen months, Secretariat started twenty-one times, won sixteen and finished in the money in all but his first race. He was an odds-on favorite seventeen times, winning thirteen. By the time he went to stud, he had won back-to-back Horse of the Year awards.

In stud, Secretariat sired such future champions as 1988 Preakness and Belmont winner Risen Star and 1986 Horse of the Year Lady's Secret. But none of his offspring came close to matching the standard he had set. He remained a popular figure even after Secretariat mania subsided. But his life ended tragically. Suffering from laminitis—a painful hoof disease—the nineteen-year-old superstar was given a lethal injection on October 4, 1989, at Claiborne Farm in Paris, Kentucky.

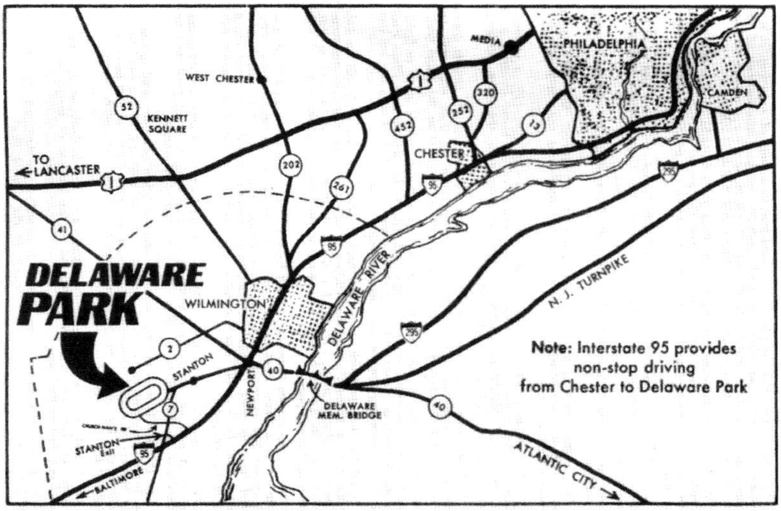

``Map of Delaware Park region, from 1970 program.

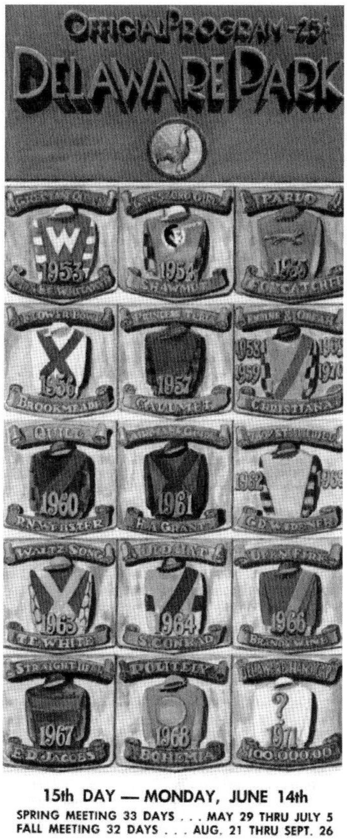

Program, 1971 session.

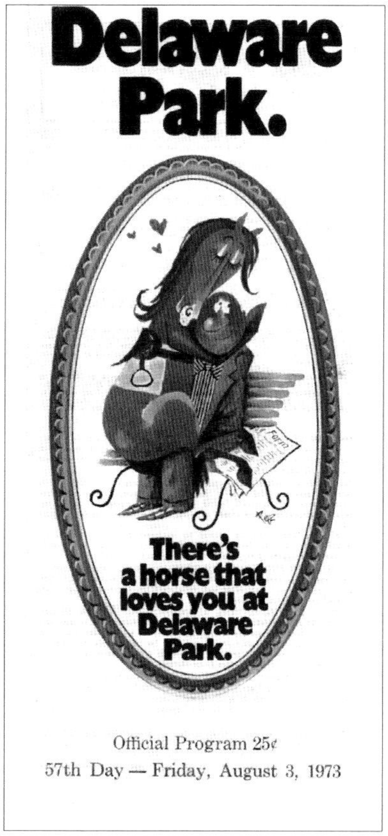

Program, 1973 session.

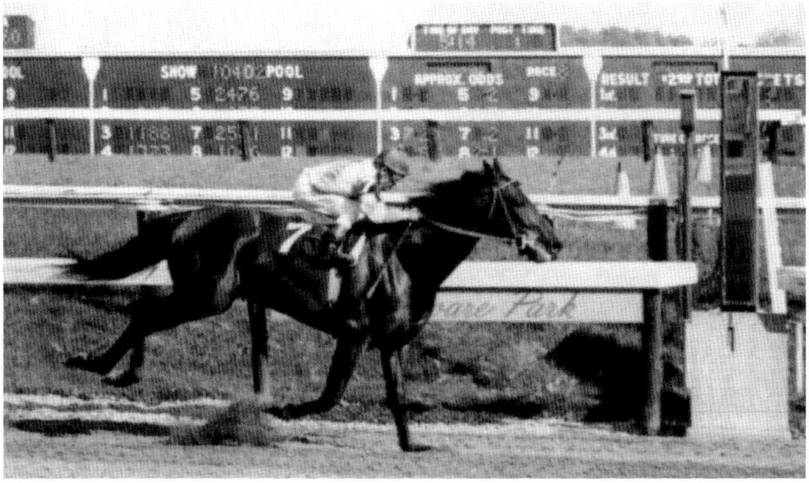

Christiana Stables' Light Hearted beating Barely Even in the 1973 Endine Handicap.

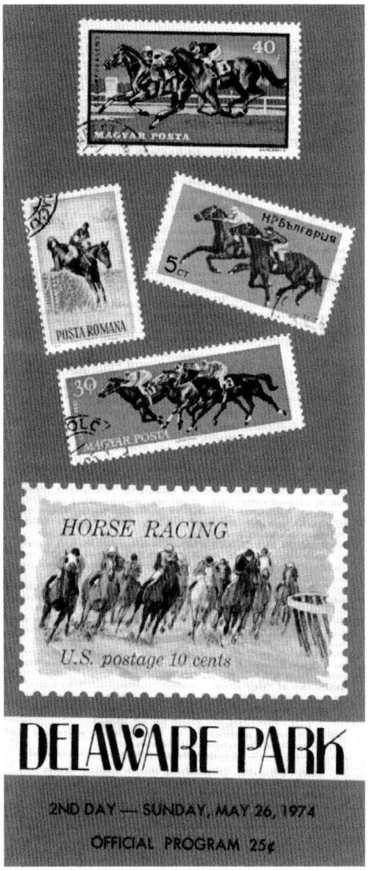

Program, 1974 session.

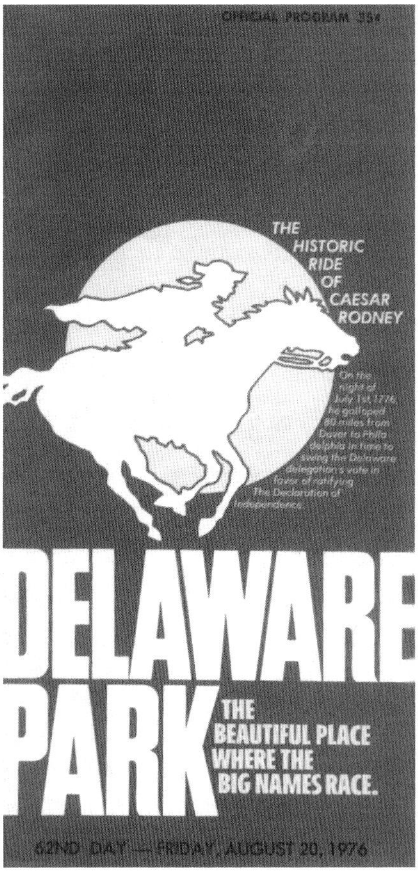

Program, 1976 session.

By mid-decade, the country turned its focus to the celebration of its own two hundredth anniversary. One of the events scheduled for this celebration was called the American Freedom Train. Local residents may remember when the train pulled into Delaware Park at the beginning of its eighteen-month tour. The triumph of the steam-powered American Freedom Train was, indeed, the only nationwide celebration of the bicentennial. It was pulled by steam locomotives in the age of the diesel, and would improve on the three display cars of its predecessor, the 1947 Freedom Train. The American Freedom Train would feature twelve display cars: ten that visitors would go aboard and pass through and two to hold large objects that would be viewed from the ground through huge "showcase" windows. The display cars were filled with over five hundred precious treasures of Americana. Included in these diverse artifacts were George Washington's copy of the Constitution, the original Louisiana Purchase, Judy Garland's dress from *The Wizard of Oz*, Joe Frazier's boxing trunks, Martin Luther King's pulpit and robes and even a rock from the moon.

Including the display cars, the American Freedom Train (AFT) was a twenty-six-car train led by one of three enormous steam engines restored just for the occasion. Over a twenty-one-month period from April 1, 1975, to December 31, 1976, more than seven million Americans visited the train during its tour of all forty-eight contiguous states. Tens of millions more stood trackside to see it go by. It was by far the greatest event on rails since the end of the steam era, and it served as the uniquely magnificent vehicle that brought America's bicentennial celebration to the people.

The twenty-six car steam-powered American Freedom Train opened to a sellout crowd of forty thousand at Delaware Park. Traffic backed up for miles on the Kirkwood Highway, and when entrance was finally achieved, hopeful visitors encountered

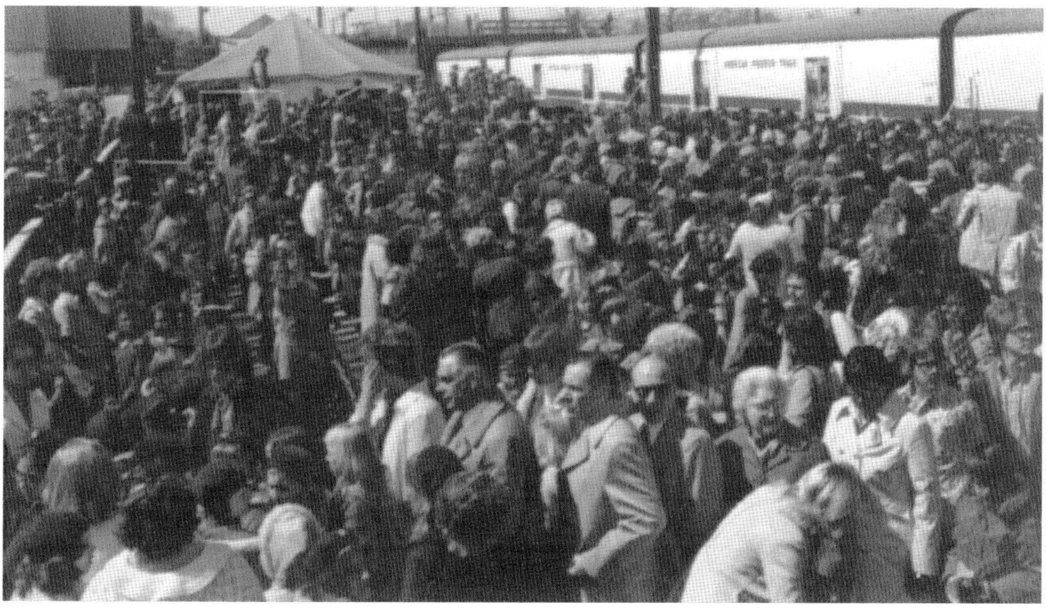

Large crowds were at every place the American Freedom Train stopped.

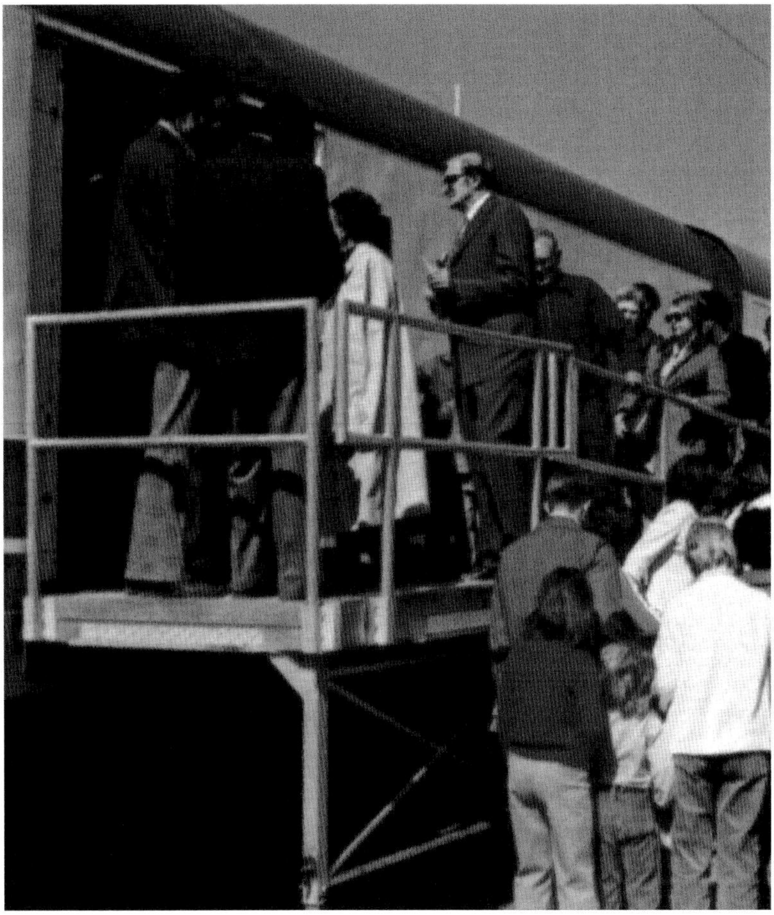

Left: Patrons file through the exhibits on the Freedom Train.

Below: Inaugural day postage cover, Delaware Park, April 1, 1976.

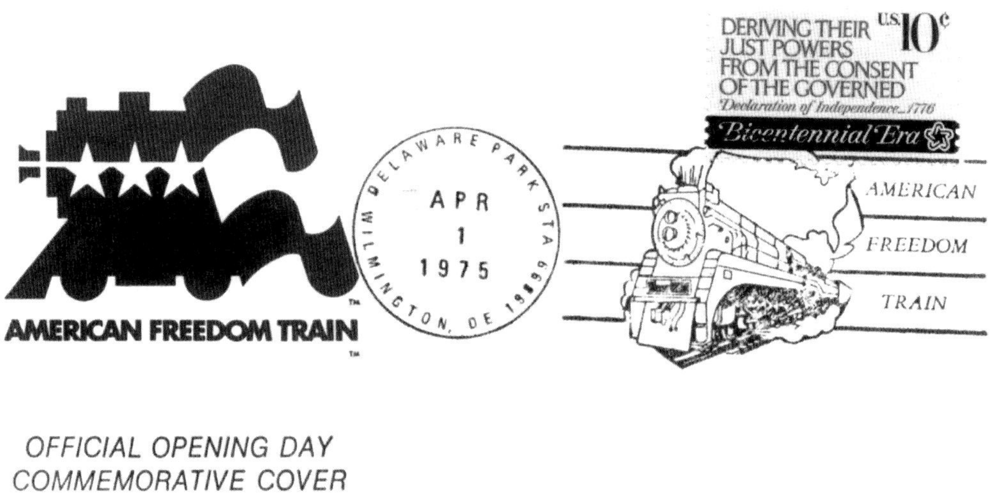

difficulties in parking and massively long lines. Opening day was not without incident, for when Governor and Mrs. Sherman Tribbett entered the train as the first visitors, the conveyor belt and the lights abruptly shut down. It seems that someone had forgotten to fuel the diesel engines that powered the train![119]

When the displays were again running, the crowds began to pour through the train on conveyor belts, too quickly for many to enjoy the displays after waiting for so long. Admission was free until noon, but this was soon extended to cover the entire day. The train displayed in Delaware Park from April 1 to April 4 and then moved under cover of night to its next destination at Albany, New York.

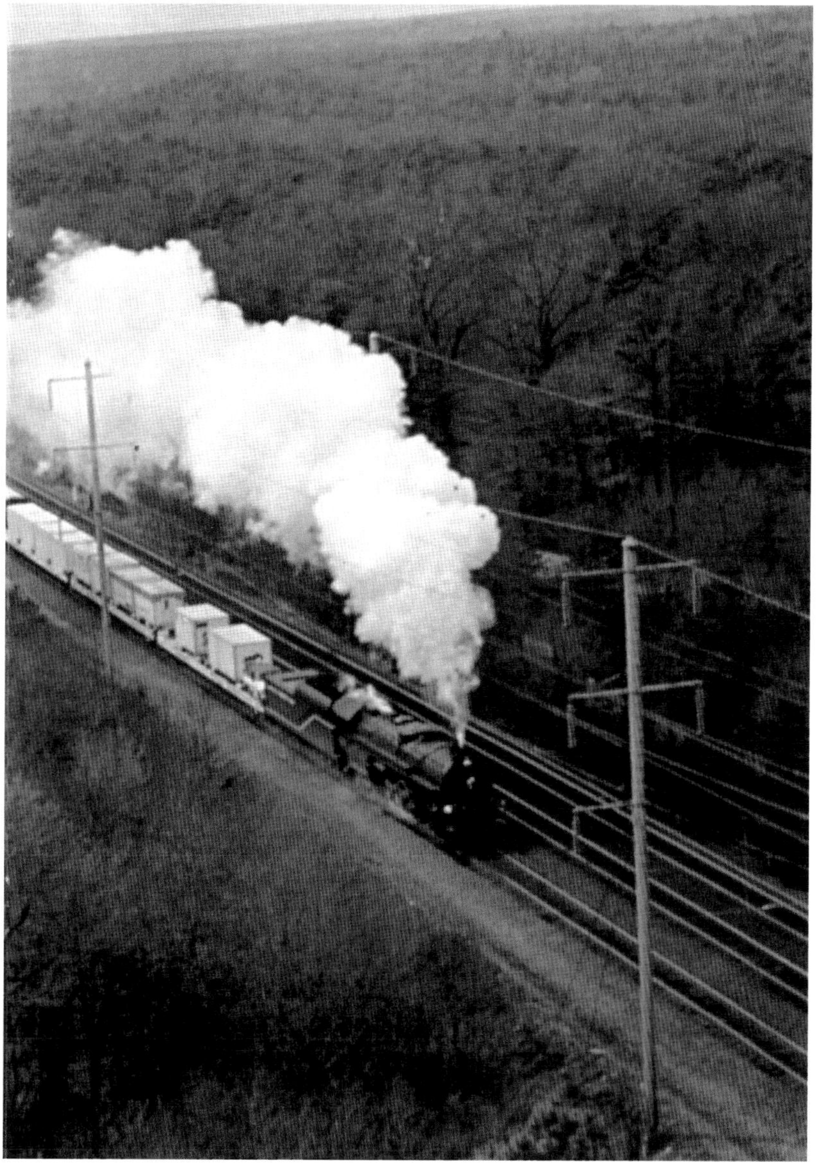

The American Freedom Train, en route to its next stop.

Tragedies at the Park

He who would venture nothing must not get on a horse.
—old Spanish proverb

It would be unfair to history to omit or gloss over the occasional tragedies that have occurred at Delaware Park. Horse racing, like any other sport, has a fine line between success and failure, and sometimes, in a split-second error, great tragedies can occur.

The first one of note happened in 1950. Richard Rozelle, twenty-two, was thrown from his horse, Raise You, in the stretch drive of the Kirkwood Purse on June 4, 1951. Junior Nurse, running behind Raise You, stumbled over the horse, but rider Joseph Dyer wasn't injured. Rozelle unfortunately was taken to the hospital with a severe skull fracture and died in the hospital.[120]

On June 2, 1959, two horses were killed and their jockeys injured in a freakish collision during their warm-up just before the seventh race. The horses, Die Valkyrie with Paul Bohenko up, and King's Chapel, with Sam Boulmetis aboard, ran head on into each other. Die Valkyrie, owned by Mrs. Helen Murrell, died almost instantly. Soon afterward King's Chapel, owned by Robert J. Ashton, died on the track. Both jockeys were taken to Delaware Hospital in Wilmington. Bohenko suffered a possible fractured nose and had several broken teeth. He was detained for X-rays, but his condition was not serious. Boulmetis was treated for bruises of the left arm and then released.[121]

On June 10, 1965, four jockeys were injured, three seriously, in two spills at Delaware Park. Raymond Kimball suffered a broken back in the fourth race when his horse, Swordman, stumbled and fell about an eighth of a mile out of the gate. Thankfully, at least, he fell away from all the other horses on the track. In the next race, Jockey Bob Corle, on Longwood Lady, was caught in tight quarters attempting to take a tight hold of the mount around the far turn. Be Alert, ridden by James Gonzalez, clipped the heels of Longwood Lady and went down, falling to the outside away from the rail. Lucies Deedes, with Ron Witmer in the saddle, fell over Be Alert, as did Fireplace, ridden by Keith Stuart. Witmer suffered only lacerations, but Stuart suffered multiple fractures and Gonzales sustained a concussion.[122]

Then, in 1968, one of those heartbreaking moments in horse racing occurred at a local stable, when the barn owned by Edward P. Taylor at his Windfield's Farm burned to the ground and killed eleven thoroughbred mares. "The greatest loss of breeding stock ever suffered in the state of Maryland," Byran Field, vice-president of Delaware Park, said of the tragedy. Three of the thoroughbreds killed in the fire were sired by Native Dancer, Maryland's famous "Grey Ghost," who had died the previous November after an operation. Native Dancer was the grandsire of Northern Dancer, winner of the 1964 Preakness and Kentucky Derby. In addition to the three in foal by Northern Dancer, another of the mares was in foal by Nearctic, Canada's horse of the year in 1967.[123]

Another notable accident occurred at the park on November 5, 1999, when three exercise riders were injured while they were breezing horses and collided with a loose horse running in the opposite direction. On November 5, Leah Waldman (a horse exerciser), Eric Jones (a self-employed jockey) and Roberto Montiel (a jockey and exercise rider) were "breezing" three race horses on the Delaware Park track around 8:30 a.m. That day the breezing consisted of the three horses bearing the aforementioned riders lining up in the starting gate and "breaking," or starting to run as soon as the gates opened. Although horses are sometimes timed during these breezes for several reasons, including publication in race-related periodicals, the record indicates that this breeze was not timed. The horses were then ridden at a very fast pace, albeit not quite as fast as in an actual horse race, once around the race track. According to the breeze riders, the purpose of that activity was to exercise the horses' muscles and to accustom the horses to running in close proximity to one another without being frightened. They were not racing; they were exercising the horses as a part of a morning workout.

A short time after the November 5 breeze began, another horse on a different part of the track broke away from its rider and ran toward the three horses being breezed. The breeze riders were injured when their horses collided with the stray horse. A fifth horse carrying an "outrider" who'd ridden over in an attempt to head off the horse that had broken away was also involved. The breeze riders suffered injuries of varying degrees. Delaware Park outrider Joe Shelton said it felt like he had been shot out of a cannon. Shelton was among four riders involved in that collision. Three horses—Shelton's mount Red Fred, Foxy Pine Ridge and Stanley's Prospect, the loose horse—were humanely destroyed on the track shortly after the accident. Four riders were injured and taken to nearby Christiana Hospital. Shelton broke his right leg in three places. Jockey Eric Jones injured a shoulder, jockey Roberto Montiel fractured his right knee and exercise rider Leah Waldman broke her left wrist and was suffering breathing problems.[124]

They were initially refused insurance benefits from the accident, and they sued the race park, which claimed coverage under an umbrella insurance policy that excluded coverage for "practicing or participating in horseracing." A court proceeding followed to determine whether the practice riders were covered under the general umbrella policy for the racetrack. The trial court opinion concluded that since the policy is ambiguous, the issue must be resolved against the insurance company, which drafted the policy and must bear responsibility for the ambiguities in it. Accordingly, it found in favor of the exercise riders.

In 2000, a fire in the grandstand forced the evacuation of hundreds of people from the slots hall. On March 23, firefighters responded to an alarm and arrived shortly before 9:00 p.m. to find smoke coming from the grandstand and the building's roof, Mill Creek Fire Company spokesman Jon Stewart said. "I was sitting inside when the buzzer went off," patron Mary Wyne said as she clutched about $100 worth of coins in a Delaware Park cup outside the hall. "They told us to clean out the machines and get out."

After an investigation, the state fire marshal's office determined that the fire was set deliberately. Assistant state fire marshal Willard F. Preston III said the blaze broke out in the roof area of the grandstand at the park's racetrack-slots casino, near Christiana Hospital. The building's alarm system activated, and the two thousand patrons were evacuated safely. Ten employees who tried to extinguish the blaze were treated at Christiana Hospital for minor smoke inhalation. Preston said an investigation determined the fire was the result of someone intentionally igniting flammable materials. Preston would not say if there were suspects. Damage, estimated at $5,000, was confined to a vacant room.[125]

Death, Resurrection and a Horse We All Loved

And it's run for the roses
As fast as you can
Your fate is delivered
Your moment's at hand
It's the chance of a lifetime
In a lifetime of chance
And it's high time you joined
In the dance
It's high time you joined
In the dance
–Dan Fogelberg, "Run for the Roses"

Aggressive racetrack development at other locations again threatened the survival of Delaware Park in the late 1970s, which had been struggling with only marginal profits ever since the expansion of racetracks in the mid-1950s.

Delaware Park's marketing area was reduced to one-fifth of any nearby racetrack. Surrounding tracks all had at least one major city and three major counties nearby, each with a greater population than the entire state of Delaware. A significant decline in profits caused by the erosion of its fan base forced the track to officially close its doors on September 6, 1982.

The commencement of thoroughbred racing at Liberty Bell Park and later at Keystone Race Track had brought the competition fifty miles closer. At various times, Keystone (now Philadelphia Park) and Garden State Park raced in conflict with Delaware Park. In 1976, the last out-of-state market disappeared when Maryland added summer racing at Bowie, creating head-to-head competition during the Delaware Park meet. The decision to close, according to officials, was a result of increased competition and a poor economy, among other things.

A statement issued by the track's directors said the closing "was dictated by a number of adverse factors, including the proliferation of competing race meetings in Delaware's drawing area, the required payment of a daily parimutuel tax of $10,000 to the state,

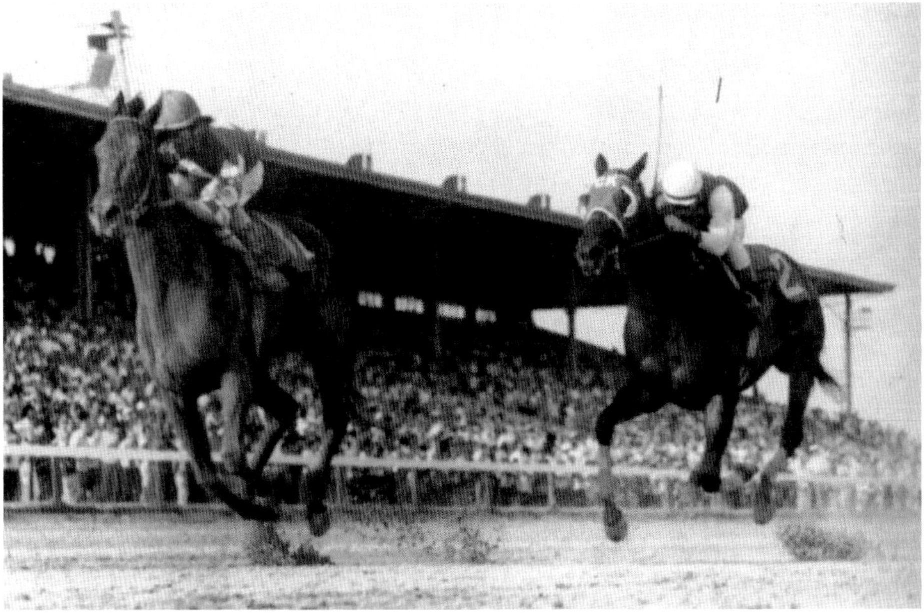

Mrs. Bertram R. Firestone's Optimistic Gal, over T.V. Vixen in the 1976 Delaware Handicap.

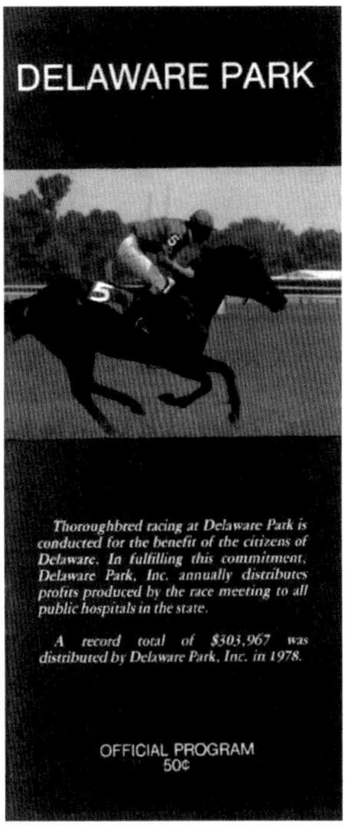

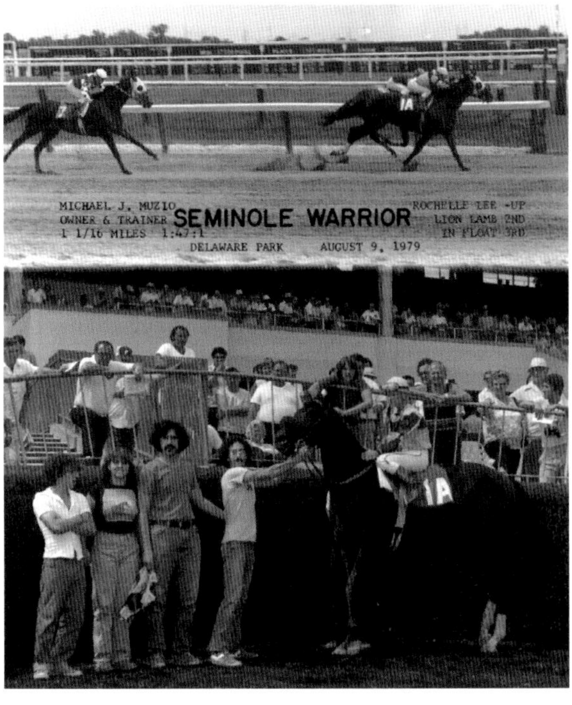

Above left: Program, 1979 session.

Above right: Seminole Warrior, winning on August 9, 1979. Michael J. Muzio, trainer, Rochelle Lee, up.

the emergence of state lotteries throughout the region, the introduction of casino gambling in Atlantic City and the unfavorable general economic climate."

Delaware Park lost money during its seventy-three-day 1982 summer meeting. The handle—the total amount wagered—was down 19.24 percent from the previous year and the horsemen received nearly $1.8 million in overpayments, track officials said. The overpayments stemmed from the track's assurance to horsemen that purses would be increased and guaranteed for the entire meeting. Delaware Park absorbed the loss. The rise in the daily purse schedule had been increased from $54,000 to $65,000 to meet the competition and attract the area's best horsemen. But the handle was not large enough to offset the huge expense. The average daily handle was $565,672, against $700,432 the previous year, coupled with an 8.43 percent decline in attendance that year.[126]

The reason for Delaware Park's failure is largely rooted in the standard for the park set by William DuPont at its inception. Not overly concerned about turning a profit, excess revenues were turned back into the park to improve the barns, the racing surfaces and the purses. If the big crowds did not provide sufficient revenue to keep the operation in the black, DuPont would simply contribute enough money out of his own pocket to keep it afloat. Of course, this funding source stopped with the death of DuPont.[127] One

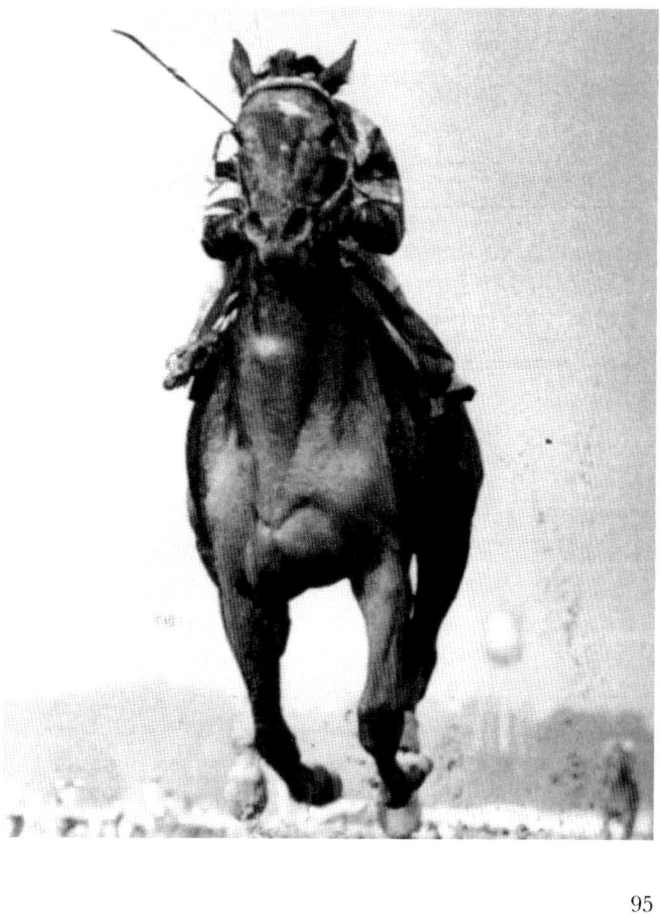

Hawksworth Farms' Spectacular Bid in the 1979 Marlboro Cup. Grover G. Delp, trainer.

local horseman stated, "Delaware Park in 1982 was overspending staggering amounts for purses. One of the great problems there was fat purses, slim fields and dull racing. It was almost as if the track was operating for the benefit of four or five horsemen."[128]

And so Delaware Park was bankrupt and shuttered, ending its forty-five-year career under the management of the Delaware Steeplechase and Race Association. In 1982, a group of developers led by former Wilmington Mayor Thomas Maloney attempted to buy the defunct park to turn it into a housing development. But although they had the financial resources behind them, the trustees refused the offer outright.

In the 1980s another major regional change occurred that impacted the park. For years, the roadways in the area had been inadequate to handle the increasing congested traffic flow. In addition, Delaware Route 7 had to pass under a narrow underpass beneath the Baltimore and Ohio Railroad line in Stanton. This underpass was subject to frequent flooding, and occasionally semi-trucks would get wedged underneath it. Traffic was bad enough as it was, but it was also announced that a portion of the Delaware Park property would be used for the construction of a new hospital to serve the suburban community.

Funds were raised in the early 1980s for a series of major traffic improvements to the area. Delaware Route 7 was dualized from the site of the projected Christiana Mall to Stanton, and the precarious underpass was replaced with the construction of a bridge over the rail lines. As the new hospital was nearing completion, toward the end of the decade, additional land was acquired and Delaware Route 4, which ran along the southern edge of the park, was dualized as well.

Fortunately, on August 28, 1983, William Christmas, a breeder with Idle Miss Farm in Monkton, Maryland, and William Rickman Sr., a Rockville, Maryland developer of office buildings, acquired most of Delaware Park. A 130-acre portion of the land closest to I-95 was reserved for the construction of the proposed hospital complex, which became the present Christiana Hospital. The developers immediately planned to install lights around the track for evening events and to winterize the barns so that longer meets could be planned. They also petitioned the state government to permit racing to begin in the spring, so they could compete with the harness racing at Brandywine Park. Throughout Delaware Park, repairs were necessary to fix the decay and damages that had occurred while the park was idled as a racing venue. Rickman stated, "It's a gamble, but I think we can do it. It makes sense to me as a businessman. And I don't do foolish things."[129] The track reopened in the spring of 1984 with a weekend-only meet ending Memorial Day. A second meet with a three-day-per-week format was attempted in the fall, but it ended prematurely due to heavy financial losses.

In the winter of 1985, William Rickman Sr. took full control of Delaware Park, determined to turn the ailing track around. The 1985 season brought moderate success to Delaware Park. The opening of the new, $180 million Garden State Park in Cherry Hill, New Jersey, had a positive impact, as the track's media blitz caused a new awareness of racing in the Delaware Valley. Also, with Garden State Park engaging in night racing, Delaware Park attracted many Philadelphia-area fans who preferred day racing. Garden State's owners, International Thoroughbred Breeders, Inc., purchased nearby Keystone Race Track and renamed it Philadelphia Park. The track, which normally opened in

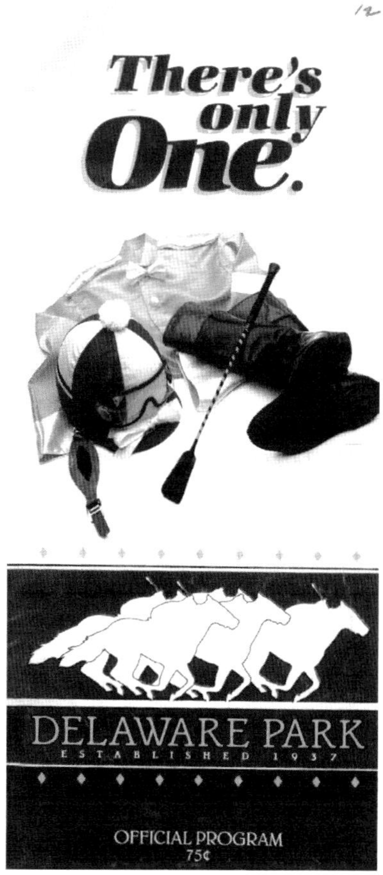

Program, 1985 session.

the summer opposite Delaware Park, remained closed until Labor Day for renovations, giving Delaware Park sole access to Philadelphia fans in the pivotal year of 1985.

The season ended with a $522,134 daily average handle. A new high mark was set for the new Delaware Park when over $1 million was wagered on Kentucky Derby day. Under the direction of William Rickman Sr., Delaware Park was successful in meeting an onslaught of competition from neighboring states over the next several years. This competition came from many directions. Philadelphia Park began a network of off-track betting parlors, bringing racing action to sites only thirty miles from Delaware Park. The Pennsylvania track also initiated telephone wagering via cable television. Fans residing just seven miles from Delaware Park could watch and wager on the races from their homes in Pennsylvania.

Garden State Park also made changes in its schedule that conflicted with Delaware Park. They included the start of Sunday racing and moving weekend racing to daytime for several years, resulting in three tracks within a sixty-mile radius operating at once (and if Maryland is included, four tracks within seventy-five miles).

Delaware Park responded with force to counter this "war" on racing markets. Track general manager John E. Mooney adopted the successful Twin Trifecta wager from

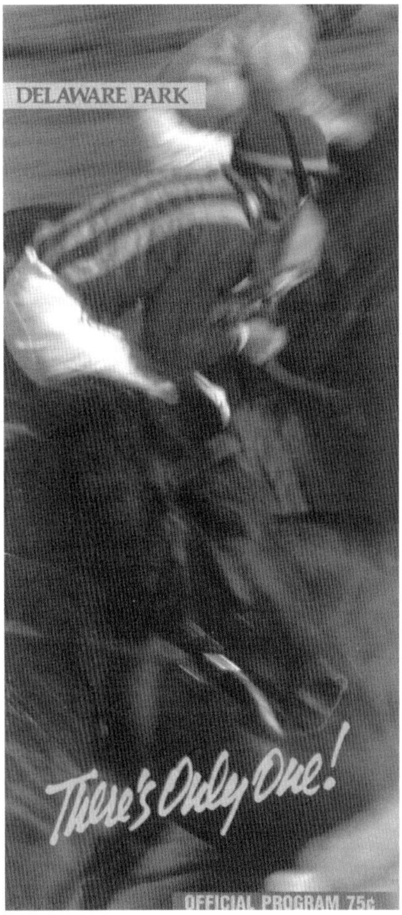

Program, 1986 session.

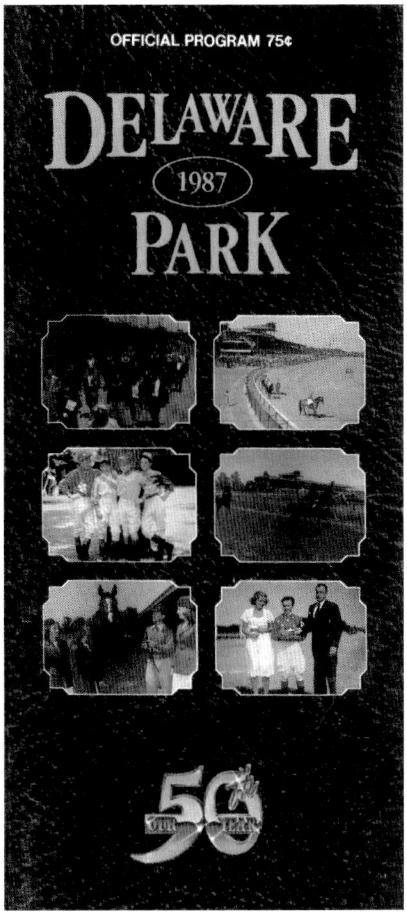

Program, 1987 session.

Suffolk Downs, becoming the first area facility to offer the exciting wager. A then-record payoff of nearly $700,000 generated massive publicity and let fans know that Delaware Park was still on the map. Delaware Park took advantage of its trackside picnic grove by developing a series of family-oriented promotions that was successful in attracting a new breed of fan. The track took a page from amusement parks and minor league baseball by opening its doors for local area entertainment.

The historic Stanton track continued its aggressive approach by encouraging Arabian racing to come to Delaware, which not only helped fill the racing cards but also attracted a new interest in racing as a whole. In 1986, former track chairman Baird Brittingham was instrumental in bringing back the prestigious Delaware Handicap, which had been moved to Saratoga after the 1982 closing of Delaware Park.

Racing in the 1980s was also assisted by the attention given to a Puerto Rico–born jockey who achieved legendary status for his racing achievements: the great Angel

Cordero Jr. In 1974, Cordero won the best-known horse race in North America, the Kentucky Derby, aboard Cannonade. Cordero won the prestigious Derby two additional times, earning a ranking of fourth in Kentucky Derby history for jockeys with multiple victories. The second win, in 1976, was with Bold Forbes. The thoroughbred was heralded as the "Puerto Rican Wonder Horse." Cordero's third Kentucky Derby win was in 1985 aboard Spend a Buck. He also won the Belmont Stakes on Bold Forbes in 1976, and he took the Preakness twice—in 1980 on Codex and in 1984 on Gate Dancer.[130]

In 1987, a large crowd appeared at Delaware Park to watch the champion jockey ride to his 5,998th victory. A week later, "Angel Cordero Jr. today became only the fourth jockey to win 6,000 races, at Monmouth Park, NJ."[131] When Cordero retired in 1990, he had racked up a total of 7,057 wins in his career, and is rated as the sixth-best jockey of all time. In his career, Cordero won a record of over $5 million.

As the park entered the 1990s, it continued to be a local favorite. Although the track's bottom line was marginal, it surprised most skeptics by outdrawing its competition on most days when all were in operation. In the summer of 1993, William Rickman Jr. took the day-to-day reins of the racetrack from his father. Delaware Park concentrated on offering local fans a schedule of multiple racing choices and created a comfortable atmosphere to watch simulcasting year-round. By mid-season, Delaware Park began sending its simulcast signal to other tracks and OTBs throughout the country.

A lion's share of the success on the track at that time was attributed to Tim Ritchey, who spent his life riding and training horses, for a time at the old Liberty Bell Park in Philadelphia and then later at Penn National. He moved to Delaware Park in 1993, and has been a leading trainer there five times. His graded stakes winners include Cat Be Nimble, Fancy Freda and Smart Guy (winner of the Pennsylvania Derby). He also campaigned stakes winner Marciano and won the Maryland Million Classic three consecutive years beginning in 2001, twice with Docent. "I stay in Delaware and run in Pennsylvania, West Virginia, New York, New Jersey," he said. "My main stable is between 45 and 50 head at Delaware Park."

In 1995, Delaware Park began a major promotional campaign to increase the number of tracks receiving its signal during the live meet. Total handle for the 1995 live racing season soared to an all-time record of $91 million. Purses for live racing, which a year earlier had been $48,000 per day, were increased several times and reached an impressive $92,000 daily at the end of the live meet. That figure was similar to Philadelphia Park and ahead of Garden State.

While the track's simulcast operation continued to grow, William Rickman Jr. personally took charge of efforts to seek video lottery legislation. Although gambling had flourished in nearby Atlantic City since the mid-1970s, it would take another twenty years to convince Delaware citizens of the benefits of legalizing gambling in the state—a throwback to the prohibitive attitudes that had kept horse racing itself from fans in Delaware for more than one hundred years. After months of strong lobbying, in June of 1994 the Delaware General Assembly passed H.B. 628, "The Horse Racing Redevelopment Act," legalizing slot machine gambling at Delaware racetracks. Under

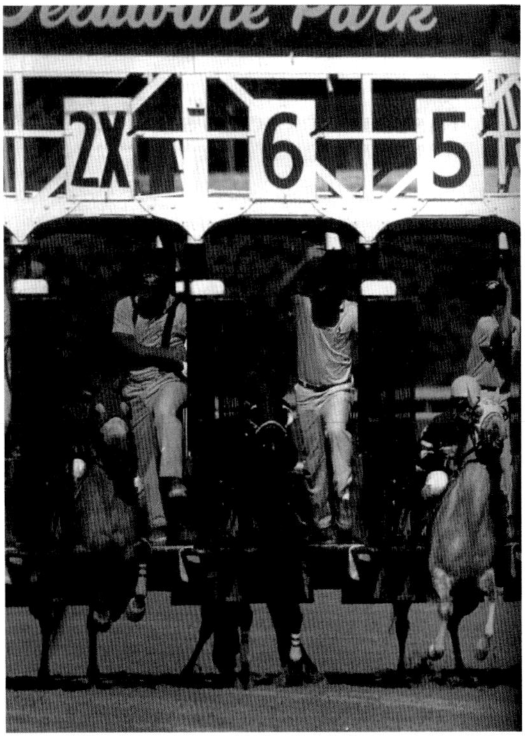

Out of the gate, Labor Day, 1991.

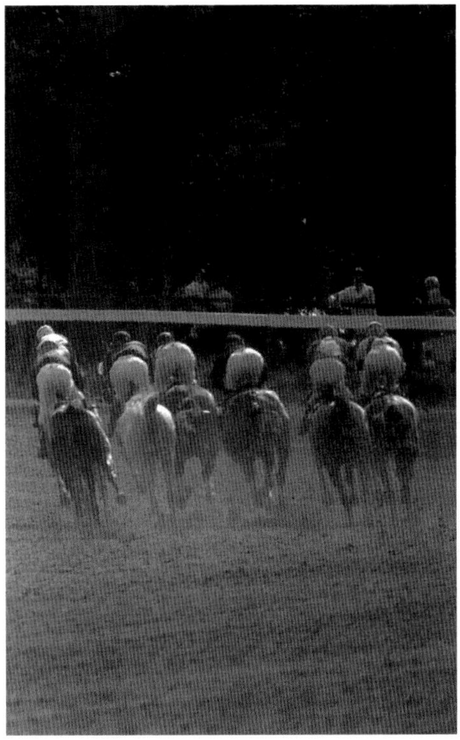

On the race, Labor Day, 1991.

the direction of the Delaware State Lottery, legislation was enacted to introduce slots at Delaware Park, Dover Downs and Harrington Raceway. Fueled with new optimism, William Rickman Jr. began the plans to make Delaware Park a major league entertainment complex.

On December 29, 1995, Delaware Park opened a slots facility, which further expanded the park's onsite attractions.

> *Delaware Park is undergoing a renaissance. The purses for which owners, trainers and jockeys compete are twice what they were a year ago. In turn, the quality of horses has increased significantly; the racing is better than in Pennsylvania and has nearly caught up with Maryland, two neighboring rivals. The reason for this apparently incongruous scene is found only a few yards away from those empty seats. On the inside of the second floor of the grandstand, in a newly carpeted room framed by oak paneling and cooled by air conditioning, are 715 slot machines, and nearly every one of them is taken. The sound of coins jingling into the air might strike a sour note with racing's purses, but for Delaware Park, it is an overture.*[132]

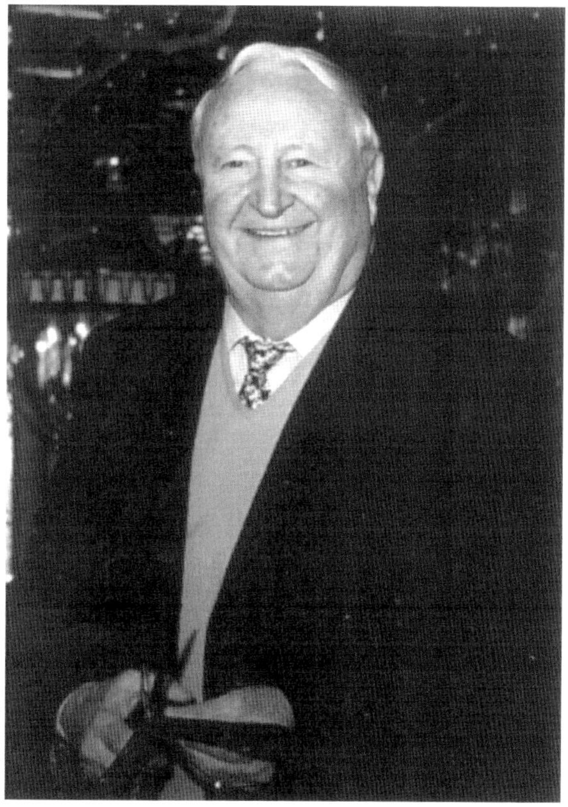

Bill Rickman, the new president of Delaware Park. *1999 Delaware Park Media and Record Guide.*

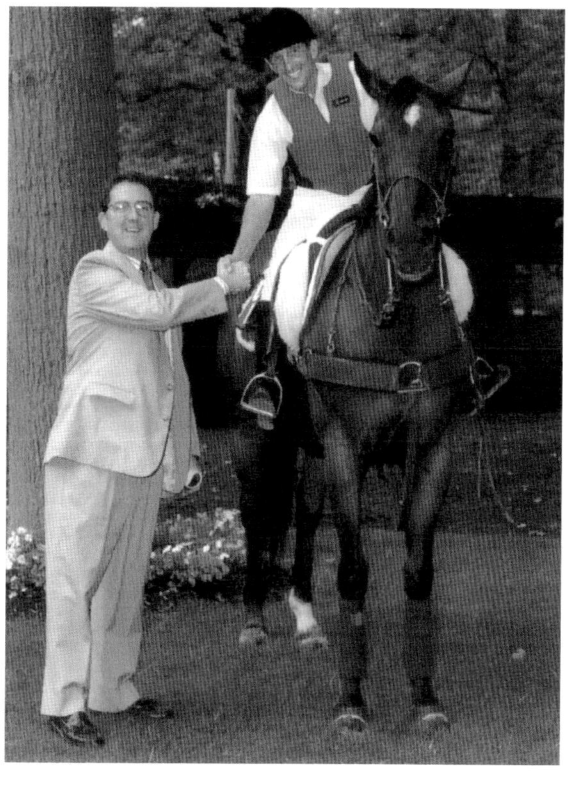

Bill Fasy, general manager, with lead outrider Steve Kisielewski. *1999 Delaware Park Media and Record Guide.*

The new slots facility was immediately successful.

> *A portion of the proceeds from the slots helps finance the track's purses, and has brought Delaware Park back from the dead. Since opening on December 29, more than $458 million has been put through the machines, and more than $3.7 million has gone to purses. Profits also go to the state, to the track and to pay for the leases on the slot machines. The venture has been so successful for Delaware Park that the $18 million debt incurred to renovate the area housing the slot machines will be retired in August, after just eight months of operation.*[133]

Rich Glazier, host of Delaware Park's simulcast broadcast show, said, "People did not want to see this track close. Here's a real strong feeling for it in the community. When you walk around here, people say, 'How's our handle?' The people have adopted the track." The managements at Delaware Park and Prairie Meadows say they could not survive without legislation permitting slots. "No question about it, it was a do-or-die situation," said William Rickman Jr., Delaware Park's president and general manager. "If the slot bill hadn't passed, we were going to close the doors."[134]

The addition of slots at Delaware Park not only saved the park from an untimely death, but also provided for the expansion of horse racing. By 1999, President William Rickman Jr. was able to expand the racetrack's card. William M. Rickman Jr. said the track had an option to ask for an additional three days that would include Breeders Cup Saturday on November 6. "With the purses increasing, it becomes much more difficult to fill races," said Rickman. "There are a lot more cheaper horses out there ready to compete. In a region that has a higher quality of racing, we want Delaware Park to be on a par with surrounding tracks. We can't just keep adding days. I feel very comfortable with 139 days. Our goal is to still bring in new horses who can fit that quality."

With the success of slot machines at Delaware Park, purses have continued to escalate over the past three seasons. Delaware's average daily purse was around $156,000 at the end of the 1998 meet. Rickman bristled at the suggestion that management's number one concern was slot machines. Under legislation enacted in 1995, state racetracks cannot operate slot machines without a live racing meet. Executive Vice-President William Fasy said that more than $2 million in off-season track renovations includes construction of three new horse barns, new electrical underground wiring on the backside, a new roof on the main grandstand, a new tote board in the infield and two new starting gates. "The most important thing is to expose our simulcast signal to make Delaware Park's live racing a national attraction," Rickman said. "The slot machines are a vehicle to get us there."[135]

Once the slots had proven a success to the future of the park, there were additional benefits. In 2000, the State of Delaware expended $16 million for a new rail station for the R-2 Line of the Southeastern Pennsylvania Transportation Authority (SEPTA) from Philadelphia and a bus hub on the grounds of Delaware Park, which they named Fairplay Station. The station was designed to serve not only the park, but also the adjacent Christiana Hospital and the MBNA Bank Center.[136]

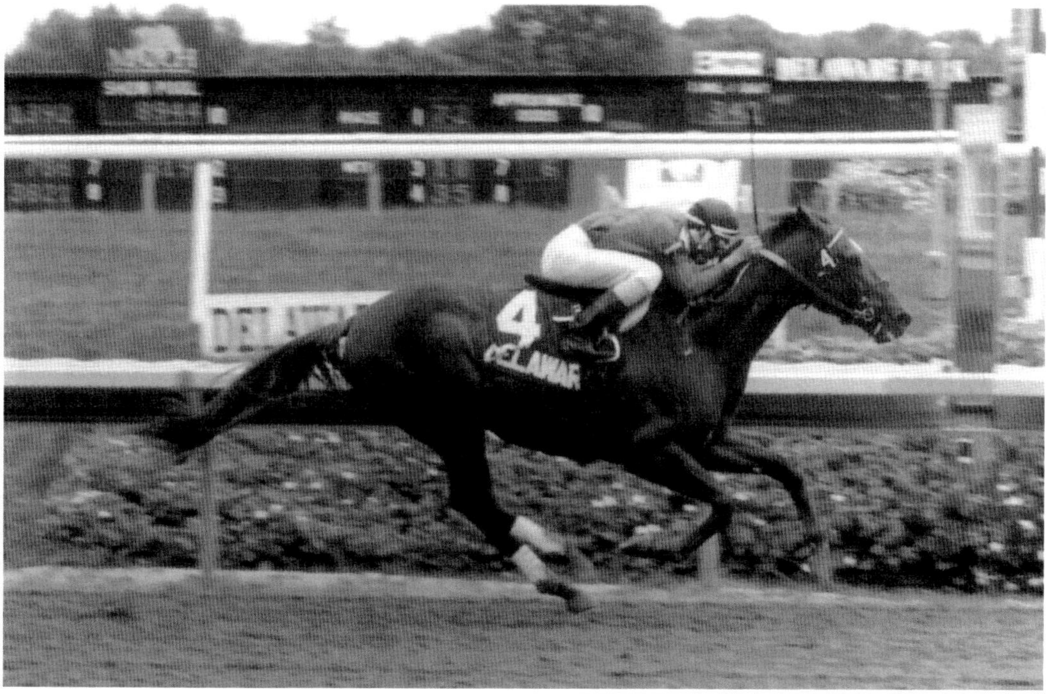

Concerto winning the 1998 Brandywine Handicap. *1999 Delaware Park Media and Record Guide.*

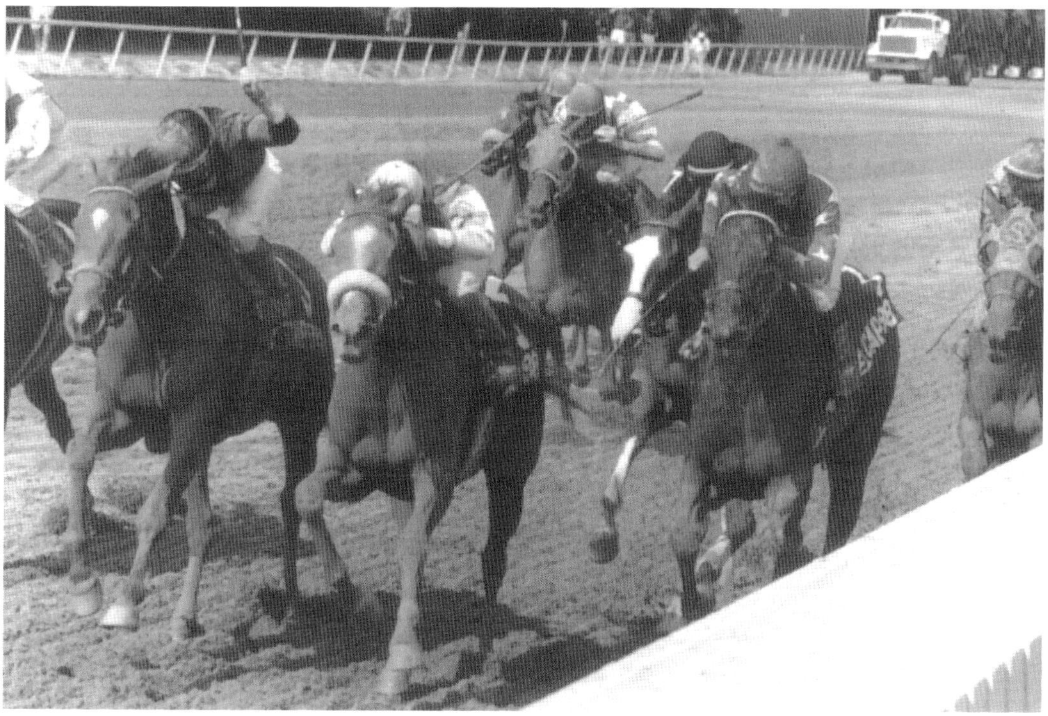

Amarillo winning the 1998 Brandywine Handicap, jockey Julie Krone. *1999 Delaware Park Media and Record Guide.*

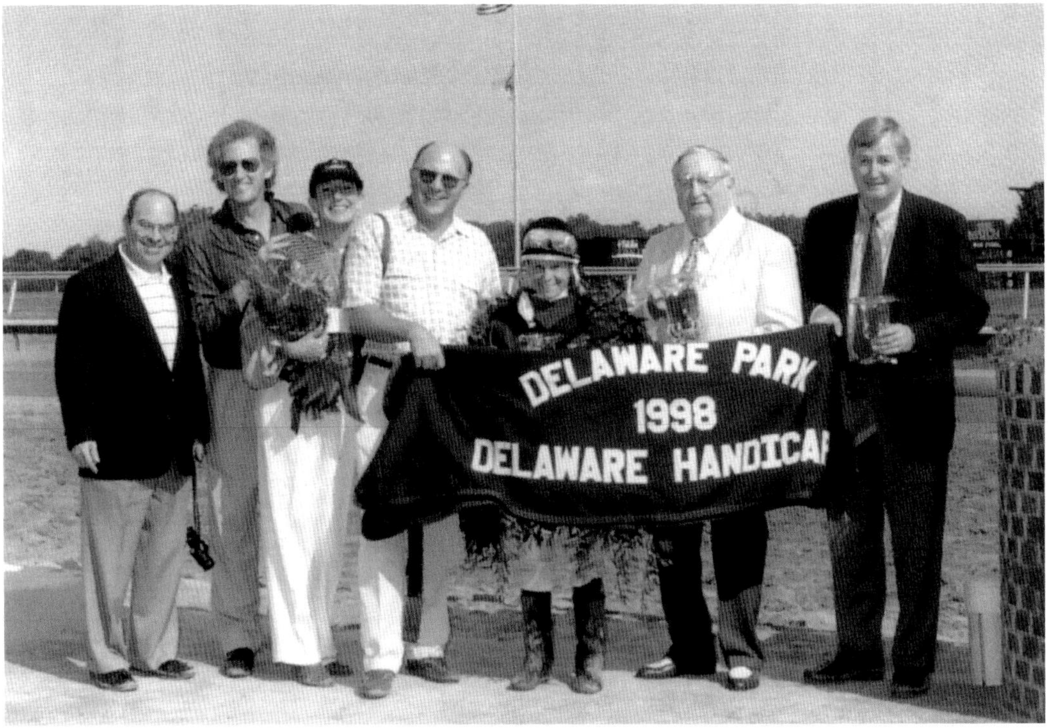

Presentation of the Brandywine Handicap trophy. *1999 Delaware Park Media and Record Guide.*

Another improvement, the result of some of the recent catastrophes at the park, was the installation of warning systems on both the main track and the training track. The systems have lights and sirens that can be activated to warn horsemen when there is a loose horse on the track. "That was a major accident we had here," said trainer Bessie Gruwell, president of the Delaware Thoroughbred Horsemen's Association, referring to the November 5, 1999 catastrophe. "I think it made everyone in the region think about what we could do to improve track safety." Gruwell said the systems have flashing lights every 1/16 of a mile, and intermittent sirens designed to let horsemen know there is a loose horse without startling other horses. "It happened about a week ago, and it worked," Gruwell said Monday. "We had a loose horse, but it only went about 1/8 of a mile before everyone knew it. I think everybody feels a lot better knowing this system is in place."[137]

Then, in 2001, Delaware Park constructed the White Clay Creek Golf Course on the property. Soon, Delaware Park was able to offer a much wider variety of entertainment for all ages and interests than ever before.

On May 7, 2001, Hall of Fame trainer D. Wayne Lukas saddled his four thousandth career winner, scoring with Added Spice in the ninth race at Delaware Park. Lukas's mark put him behind only Dale Baird (8,479 wins), Jack Van Berg (6,300) and King Leatherbury (5,190). Mr. Lukas has won 27 races worth at least $1 million and 1,052 stakes. His horses have won the Preakness on five occasions and Belmont four times, and he was the first trainer to sweep the Triple Crown with two different horses in a season.

In February of 2002, Delaware Park jockey Jeremy Rose was selected to win the Eclipse Award as the nation's top apprentice jockey. In voting by members of the Daily Racing Form, National Turf Writers Association and National Thoroughbred Racing Association, Rose beat runner-up Kris Prather by 193–28. Rose received the award at the Eclipse Awards dinner in Miami. Rose became the first Delaware Park regular to win the Eclipse as top apprentice since Juan Umana in 1993. He dethroned five-time leading rider Mike McCarthy in his first full season at Delaware Park. Rose won a Delaware Park–record 150 races, including 6 stakes, and added 117 seconds and 107 thirds in 705 mounts. He also finished second in the Meadowlands meet in East Rutherford, New Jersey, and overall won 312 races, including 10 stakes, and more than $6.6 million in purses. Rose's breakout season came after he received a call from Kid Breeden, his agent, while he was galloping horses at Gulfstream, Florida. "I'm just glad I made the call to get him up here last February," Breeden said. "Prather had something like 110 wins before Jeremy even started. His first day at Laurel, he won two of three starts. Rose rode during the day at Delaware Park and at night at the Meadowlands, two hours away. He would be back in Stanton the following day to exercise horses at 6 a.m. A tribute to his success is how he was able to ride day and night for about six weeks."[138]

A whole new generation of fans was brought into Delaware Park during the years 2005 and 2006, when two special horses with local ties brought both excitement and heartbreak to local fans. The first of these was Afleet Alex, who had won the Arkansas Derby three weeks before the Kentucky Derby by an astounding eight lengths. Local horse racing fans were all sure that Delaware Park was finally going to crown a Derby winner. It was the most attention that Delaware fans had given a single horse since Kelso raced here in the 1960s. On race day, May 7, 2005, 16,834 excited fans showed up at the park to watch the Kentucky Derby on simulcast. The local crowd rallied behind the winning horse, and the concessions sold out of Afleet Alex hats a week before the race. However, "When Afleet Alex split the horses at the top of the stretch, looming as a possible winner, many fans began screaming for the horse and jockey Jeremy Rose. But when Afleet Alex yielded to winner Giacomo and runner-up Closing Argument, the party atmosphere quickly subsided, and thousands of disappointed players headed for the exits."[139]

Perhaps drawing a more positive memory of that day was the national attention given to another Alex at Delaware Park that was featured prominently during the Derby broadcast. A local chapter of the Alex's Lemonade Stand Foundation opened a stand at the park on race day, and hundreds of the fans donated to the cause as part of the excitement prior to the race. Alex's Lemonade Stand, founded by cancer victim Alexandra Scott, became a national phenomenon for raising funds for cancer research by 2004.[140] The celebration of the two Alex's that day at Delaware Park made a lasting memory for many attendees.

Two weeks later, Afleet Alex went on to win the second leg of the Triple Crown, the Preakness Stakes at Pimlico, in a stunning victory, leaving Giacomo, winner of the Kentucky Derby, third. In his astounding Preakness victory, Afleet Alex, as well as possibly the entire field, narrowly escaped disaster when Scrappy T, who was in the lead, swung out at the top of the stretch as a result of an aggressive smack of his jockey Ramon Dominguez's whip, veering straight into Alex just as he made his move and clipping heels with him. This in turn caused Alex to stumble so badly that his jockey Jeremy Rose was thrown far over his neck, Alex nearly went to his knees and his nose came within an inch of the dirt. In a feat of never-to-be-forgotten athleticism by both horse and rider, Alex picked himself up and recovered his momentum, flying away from Scrappy T for an amazing 4¾-lengths victory. He finished the 1³/₁₆-mile distance of the Preakness in 1:55, the fastest Preakness of the past eight years, turning in one of the fastest final ³/₁₆ in Preakness history.

On September 30, 2005, William Rickman Sr. died at his home in Rockville Maryland. He had bought Delaware Park in 1983, but subsequently turned its operation over to his son, William Jr., in the summer of 1993. At Mr. Rickman's death, Delaware Governor Ruth Ann Minner stated, "Bill Rickman was a friend, as well as a prominent Delaware businessman. He has made significant contributions to our state and the Delaware horse racing industry, and he will be sorely missed."[141]

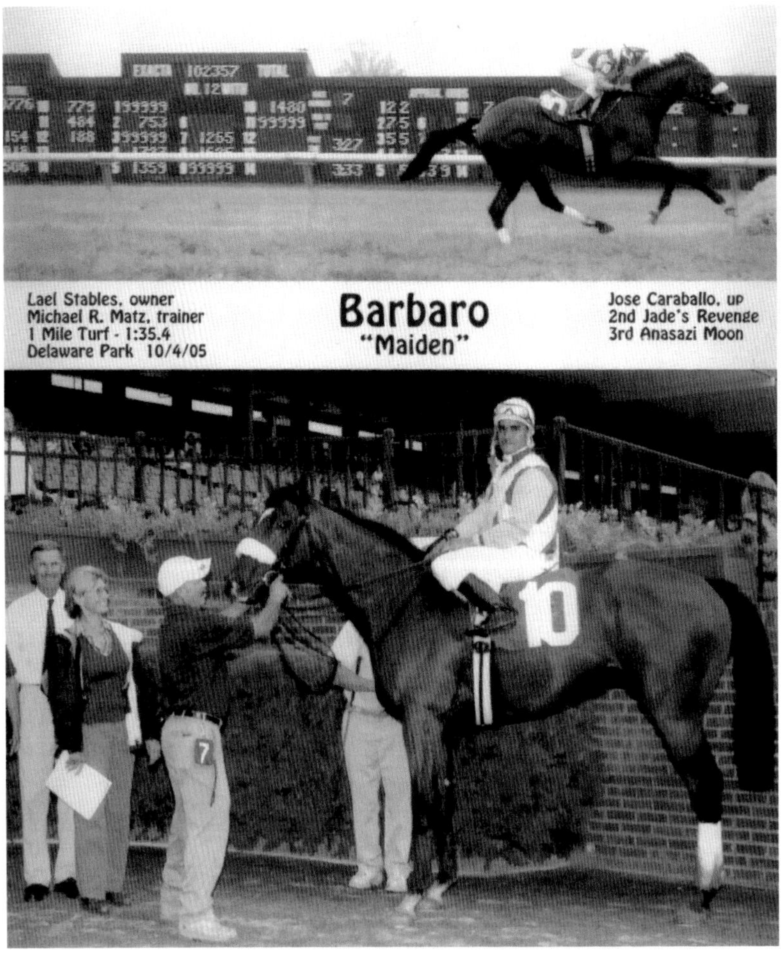

Barbaro's maiden race on October 4, 2005. Lael Stables, owner, Michael R. Matz, trainer, Jose Carabello, up.

Delaware Park again achieved national attention in 2006, when the world watched the fate of a horse named Barbaro. Trained by Michael Matz, Barbaro was a regular favorite at Delaware Park. Matz first saw the potential for the horse at Delaware. Led to the gate for the first race of his career, Barbaro shied away, reluctant to get started. A mile later, after an eye-catching 8½-length victory on October 4, 2005, at Delaware Park, trainer Michael Matz and owners Gretchen and Roy Jackson realized they might have a special thoroughbred. "He broke sharp after that, and it was just a run for fun, pretty exciting," Matz said outside his barn at the Fair Hill Training Center in Elkton, Maryland. "We knew we had a good horse."[142] Peter Brette, Matz's assistant, said that Barbaro was the horse of a lifetime. "Twenty-four years I've been riding, and he was the best. I can't imagine sitting on something as good as him."

Barbaro was a favorite in the next year's contests. On May 7, 2006, Barbaro, ridden by Edgar Prado, won the 132nd running of the Kentucky Derby at Churchill Downs. The three-year-old colt posted a 6½-length victory over Bluegrass Cat, with Steppenwolfer finishing third in the twenty-horse field. Barbaro became the second horse from the Philadelphia area to win the Run for the Roses, by the largest margin in sixty years, and excitement mounted throughout the area as a potential for the treasured Triple Crown. But fate would not be kind. Unfortunately, at the Preakness on May 20, 2006, Barbaro suffered an injury shortly after the start of the race, as he fractured three bones in and around the ankle of his right hind leg. The world was shocked, and watched and prayed for the horse's recovery.

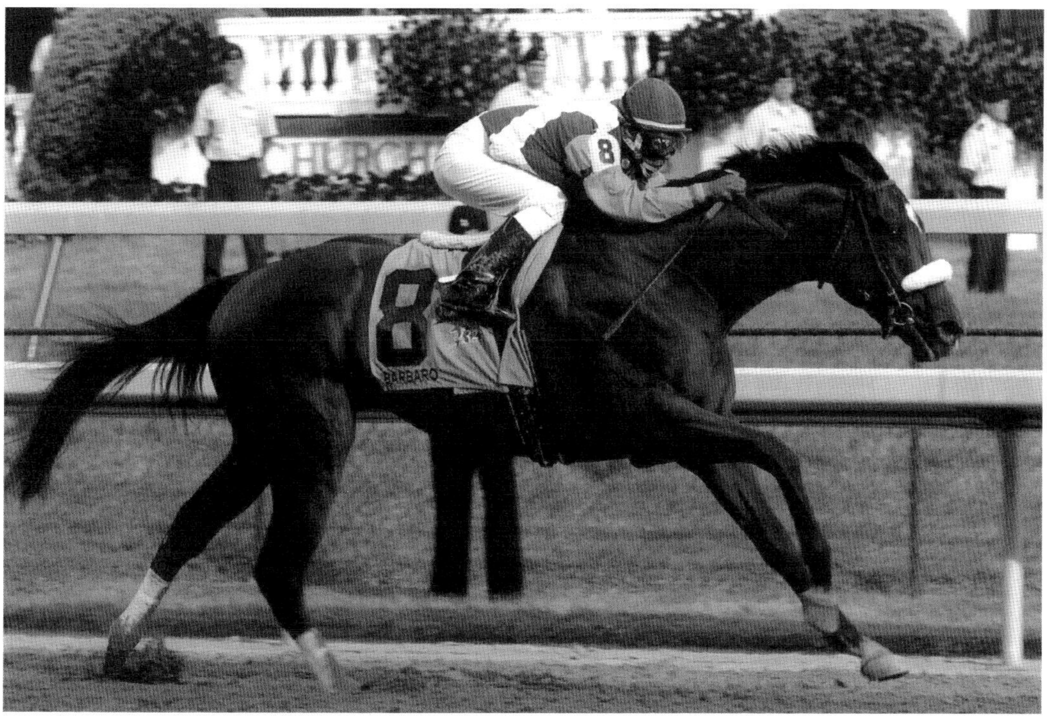

Barbaro in 2006. *Courtesy of J. Saylor.*

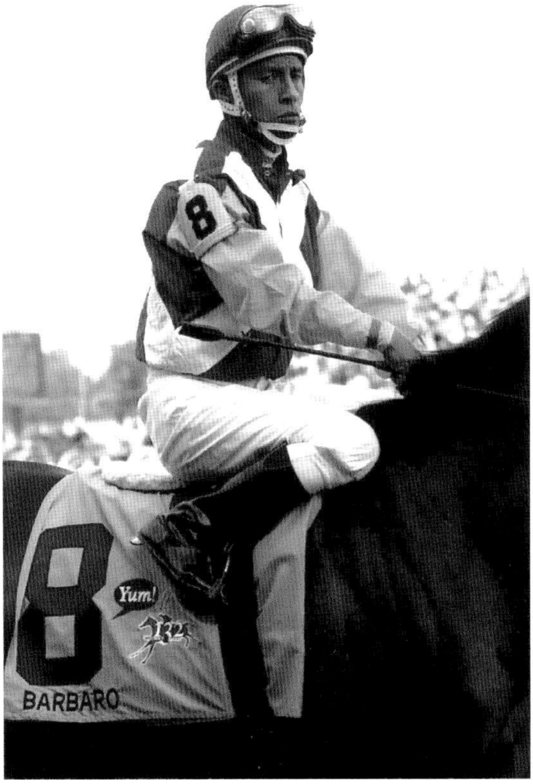

Edgar Prado on Barbaro, 2006. *Courtesy of J. Saylor.*

Although signs of a successful recovery from the injury were reported in June of 2006, Barbaro was found to have laminitis in his left hind leg, resulting in the removal of 80 percent of the hoof wall. Under the careful attention of Dr. Dean Anderson, Barbaro had to go through repeated surgeries to attempt to treat the laminitis. The world remained drawn to updates of Barbaro's health—the website of the New Bolton Center, where Barbaro was being treated, was getting up to 177,000 hits a day from concerned fans.[143]

Unfortunately, Barbaro took a significant downturn in early 2007. The cast on his leg was removed in January, and he began to show signs of discomfort. Throughout the month, it became evident that the horse was suffering more and more. On January 29, 2007, Dr. Richardson made the sad decision to euthanize the horse. "Clearly, this was a difficult decision to make," Richardson said. "It hinged on what we said all along, whether or not we thought the quality of life was acceptable. The probability outcomes was just so poor."[144] People throughout the country, and nowhere more so than at his home track, mourned the loss of this brave horse who had made a valiant effort to survive.

On April 29, 2007, six hundred members of the Friends of Barbaro met at Delaware Park to celebrate the horse's birthday in the Grove. Owners Roy and Gretchen Jackson were greeted with a thunderous ovation and presented with many memorial gifts about their ill-fated Derby horse. The Friends of Barbaro was organized by Alex Brown, an exercise rider at the Fair Hill Training Center, to raise funds for laminitis research.[145]

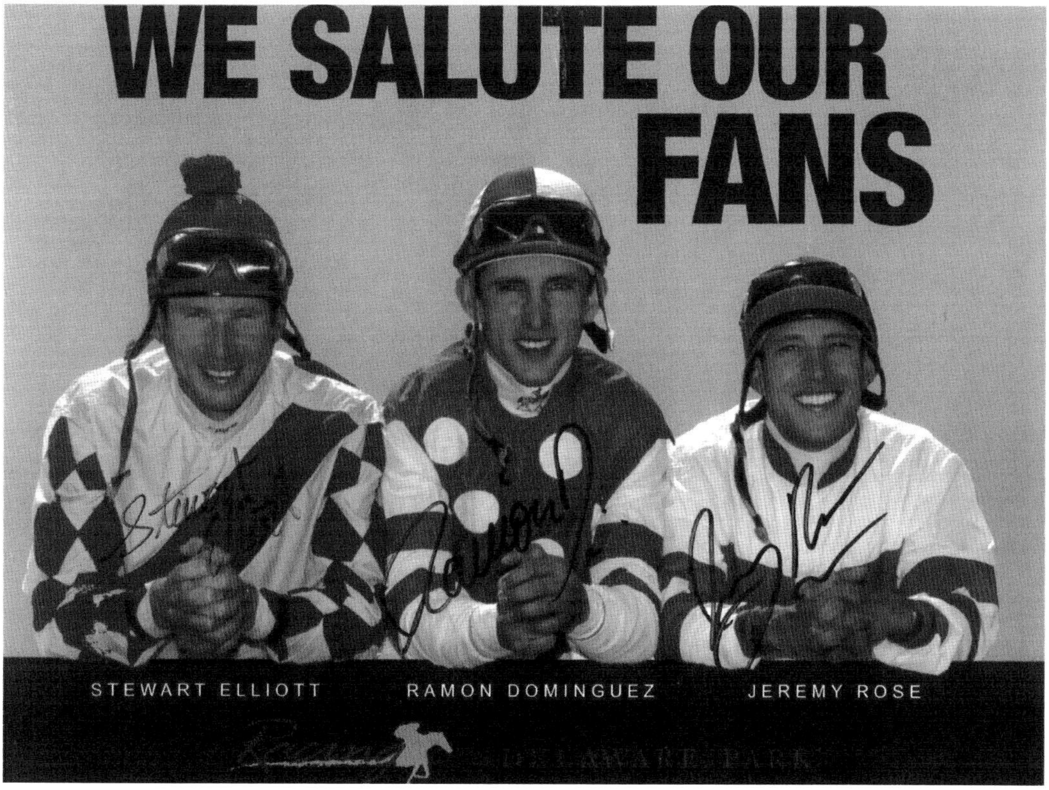

Stewart Elliott, Ramon Dominguez and Jeremy Rose on fan appreciation day, 2006.

In memory of Barbaro, Delaware Park decided in 2006 to change the name of the Leonard Richards Stakes to the Barbaro Stakes. The renamed stakes will be a grade three race for three-year-olds and will continue to offer a guaranteed purse of $300,000. The Barbaro stakes will run during Delaware Park's Delaware Handicap weekend. "Our new Racing Secretary, Ismael "Izzy" Trejo, suggested the idea of The Barbaro Stakes, and we all agreed this was a terrific way to memorialize Barbaro's legacy and to honor the Jackson family and Dr. Dean Richardson," said Bill Fasy, general manager of the park. Added Trejo, "The deep admiration and love everyone felt for Barbaro was truly overwhelming. To be able to honor such a tenaciously spirited horse, whose remarkable career started here at Delaware Park in 2005, with its own Stakes race, makes the racing family here at Delaware Park extremely proud."[146]

Meanwhile, Delaware Park celebrated the achievements of its three most famous active jockeys—Stewart Elliott, Ramon Dominguez and Jeremy Rose—by issuing a commemorative poster in August of 2006. Elliott won the Kentucky Derby and Preakness aboard Smarty Jones in 2004, and moved to Delaware in 2006. Dominguez was the leading rider at Delaware Park during the period from 2002 to 2005. Rose was the park's leading rider in 2001, won the 2005 Arkansas Derby on Afleet Alex and notched his one thousandth win aboard Mararita Maggie at Delaware Park on July 3, 2005.

Finally, Delaware Park's success was again threatened when Hannah's Resorts opened a slots gambling facility in nearby Chester, Pennsylvania in January 2007. The state predicted an expected drop in revenue of $5 million in two years due to Pennsylvania gamblers using the Chester facility instead of Delaware Park.[147] Another slots facility was established in the Poconos. Then, in 2007, it was announced that a major waterfront casino complex would be built along I-95 in Philadelphia, although considerable local objection arose against that plan. Only time will tell if Delaware Park will be able to weather this storm, as it has so many times before.

Likewise, the potential profit of racing and its benefits to the coffers of state tax rolls encouraged the state of Maryland to consider a plan to develop gambling venues at select locations in the state. The closest proposed site was to be located in the town of Perryville, Cecil County, which would attract a large percentage of the Marylanders going to Delaware Park. The Maryland legislature was not willing to formally propose the legalization of slots gambling in the state, and instead decided to put it on a public referendum for November 2008.

Another issue that arose in 2007 was the decision to regulate the use of anabolic steroids in horse racing. Arising from calamitous impacts to baseball and other sports, a model rule was developed by the Association of Racing Commissioners International and Racing Medication and Testing Consortium. On December 14, 2007, the commission's executive director, John Wayne, told the Delaware Department of Agriculture, which oversees the commission, that horsemen would be advised of the ban on anabolic and androgenic steroids. Commonly used steroids include boldenone (Equipoise), stanozolol (Winstrol), nandrolone (Durabolin) and testosterone, all of which are governed by the Racing and Medication Testing Consortium model rule being implemented in various states.[148] Delaware Park expected to begin testing for violations of the rule in the 2008 session.

On July 10, 2007, Delaware Park established its own Wall of Fame to honor some of the racing greats that touched the history of the racetrack. In its inaugural induction those selected included Kelso, Henry Clark, William Shoemaker, Christiana Stables (Jane and Henry Lunger) and William DuPont Jr. Each year the park will select one horse, trainer, jockey, owner and non-participant. "We are extremely pleased to introduce the Delaware Park Wall of Fame," said Bill Fasy, chief operating officer of Delaware Park. "With our rich racing history and tradition, it is a natural fit to establish a Wall of Fame. This allows us to recognize the truly remarkable achievements and commitment of the horsemen at our local track. This year's inaugural class represents the best of racing on both a local and national level."

Bohemia Stable's Kelso was five-time Horse of the Year from 1960 to 1964. He was owned by Allaire DuPont of Wilmington and trained by Carl Hanford. The great gelding retired from racing with a record of 39 wins in 63 starts and earnings of nearly $2 million. Willie Shoemaker rode from 1949 to 1990 and had 8,333 wins from 40,350 mounts, including winning 4 Kentucky Derbies, 2 Preakness Stakes and 5 Belmont Stakes. He was remembered locally for winning on Spectacular Bid in August of 1979 at Delaware Park after an injury at the Belmont. In that race he set a track record of 1:41 $^{2}/_{5}$ that stood for twenty-eight years. Henry Clark trained from 1929 to 1999 and

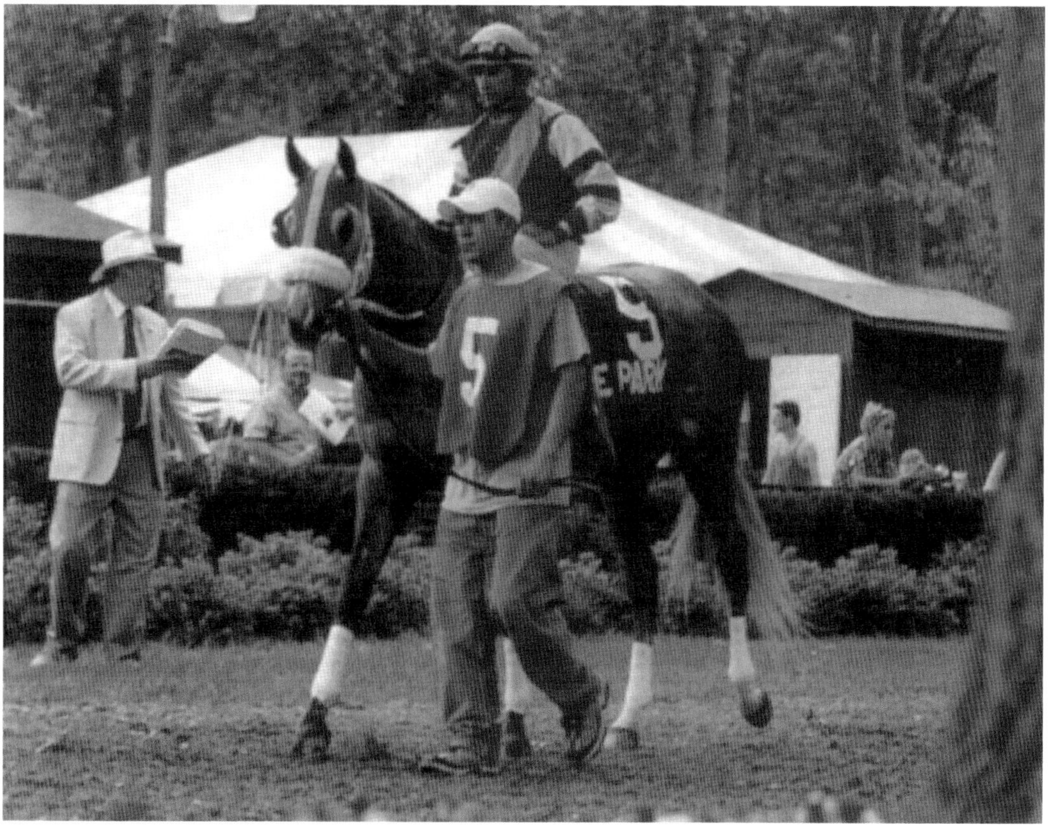

Warming the horse. *1999 Delaware Park Media and Record Guide.*

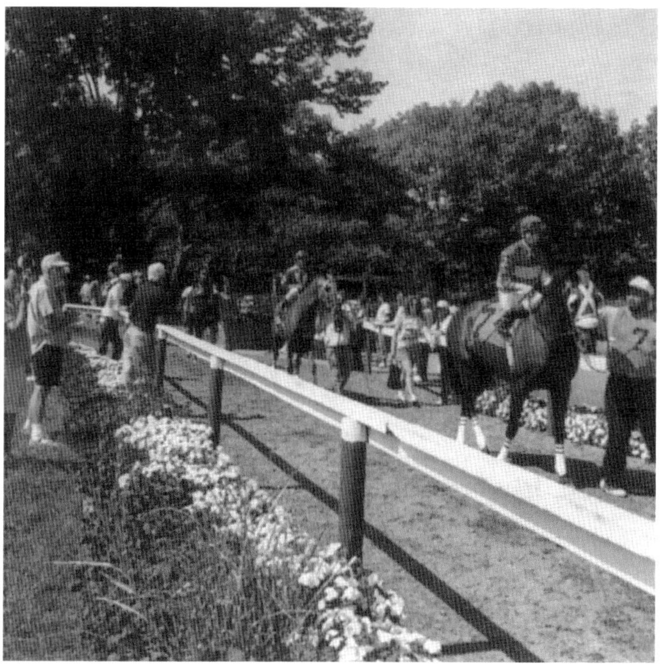

The paddock. *1999 Delaware Park Media and Record Guide.*

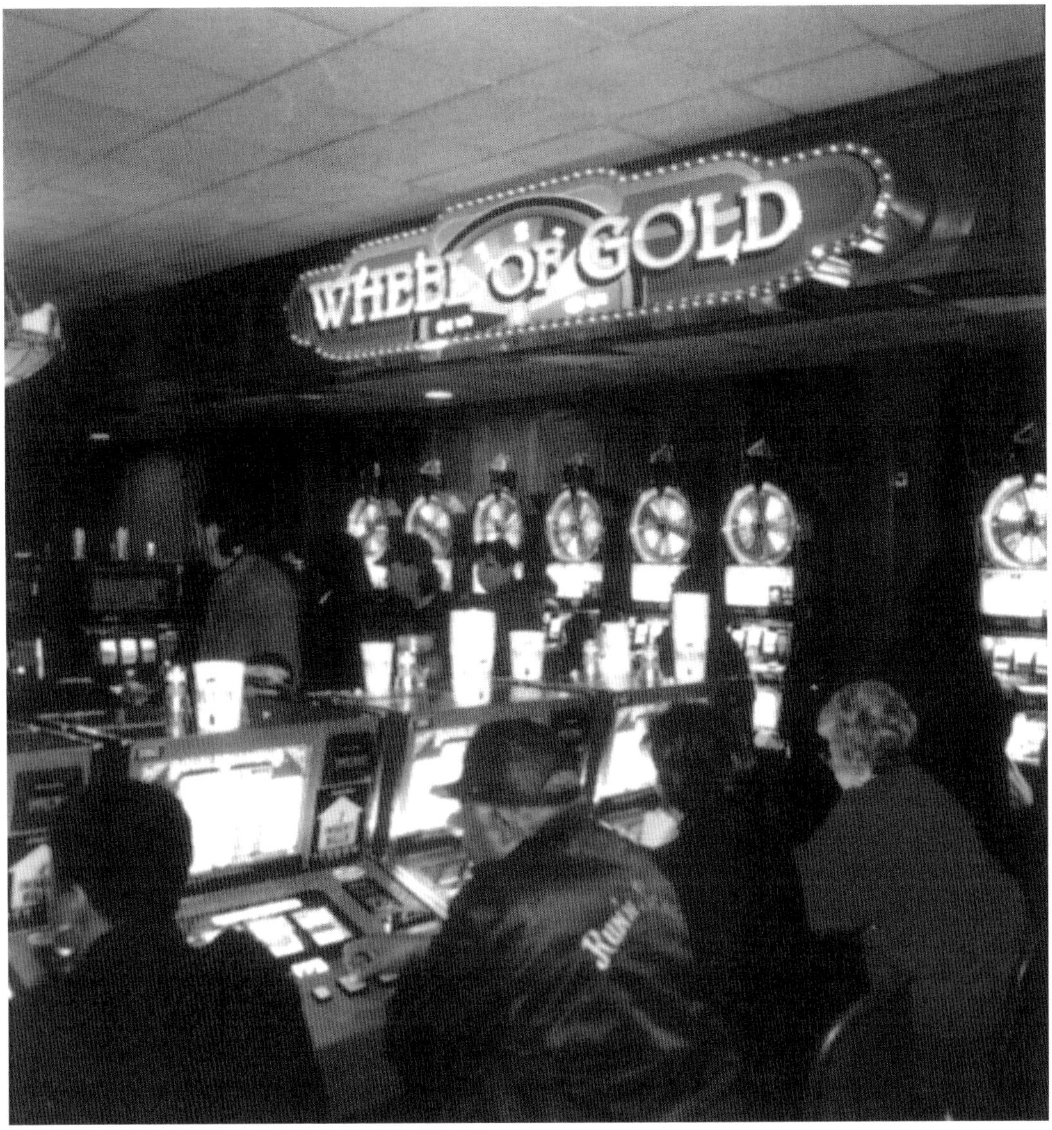

The slots hall. *1999 Delaware Park Media and Record Guide.*

had 37 stake winners. He trained both Obeah and Endine, each two-time winners of the Delaware Handicap. Christiana Stables was honored for raising a long list of champion horses, including Obeah, Stern the Tide, Under the Rug, Broom Dance and End Sweep. William Dupont, founder of Delaware Park, was honored for his idea and construction that resulted in Delaware Park itself.[149]

The 2007 session ended with a combined handle of $212 million. It was a 5.82 percent decrease from the previous year, which was attributed by Bill Fasy to a shortage of qualified horses in the area. There were, however, substantial improvements to the park, including the installation of a giant infield video monitor, renovations to the VIP room and third-floor clubhouse and various other trackside improvements.

The highlight of the session was due to the success of Delaware Park–raised Hard Spun. The three-year-old ran second in the Kentucky Derby, third in the Preakness and second in the Breeder's Cap Classic. A record handle was established at that year's Delaware Handicap Day with $4.9 million. And Scott Lake, the leading trainer in the country, scored his sixth consecutive leading trainer title by saddling ninety-seven winners.

Delaware Park also celebrated the six thousandth race of its jockey, Mario Pino. The forty-seven-year-old had won eighty-nine races and earned $2,780,965 in the 2007 session. "We are extremely excited for Mario and offer him our congratulations on this lofty achievement," stated Bill Fasy, chief operating officer for Delaware Park. "We are fortunate to have had such a high caliber of talent in our jockey colony; all of these men and women epitomize Delaware Park's grand history of racing." Pino was honored by a winner's circle presentation of a bronze horse statue and a Cartier watch.[150]

It may have been the slots that provided the financial resources to keep Delaware Park open and operating, but it was the management's continued dedication to keeping it as a friendly, enjoyable atmosphere that kept it operating as a favorite place to go. It continues to have a park-like atmosphere, inviting friends and families alike to enjoy the grounds and festivities.[151]

Whether dropping a few coins into the slot machines, watching the horses warming up in the veranda or enjoying a picnic in the grove, Delaware Park still serves the community as a pleasant place for fun and excitement. William DuPont's original vision of developing a racetrack that could attract both bettors and families alike has endured for seventy years, and I hope that it continues to maintain that tradition for years to come.

Fondly Remembered

Somewhere in time's own space
There must be some sweet pastured place
Where creeks sing on and tall trees grow
Some paradise where horses go,
For by the love that guides my pen
I know great horses live again.
–Stanley Harrison

The park was saddened when its original general manager, Edward Burke, died on January 1, 1947.[152] The mid-1960s again brought moments of tears and tragedy to the park. In June of 1965, the twenty-year career of Aloysius A. Fahey ended with his death. He had served the park since 1947, as publicity director and assistant to the racing director.[153]

On December 12, 1973, Donald P. Ross, chairman of Delaware Park racetrack, died in Wilmington at the age of seventy-one. Mr. Ross was co-founder of the thoroughbred track in 1937 and served as its president from 1946 to 1957. A former steward of the Jockey Club, Mr. Ross was also a past president of the Thoroughbred Racing Association. When the New York Board of Regents issued a charter for the National Museum of Racing at Saratoga, he was one of the original trustees.[154]

On June 30, 2000, Delaware Park mourned the loss of Donald Peabody Ross Jr. The son of Don P. Ross and Wilhelmina DuPont Ross, he followed in his father's footsteps and was a member of the Thoroughbred Racing Association, Jockey Club, National Steeplechase and Hunt Association, Farmer's Club and Wilmington Point to Point. He was also the past president of the Wilmington Club and the Vicmead Hunt Club, the Betty Ford Alpine Gardens, BRAVO and the Vail Valley Foundation.[155]

On September 18, 2001, Jane DuPont Lunger, one of the class owners in all of thoroughbred racing, died of cancer at the age of eighty-seven. Lunger, owner of the nationally known Christiana Stables, had been involved in racing since 1936. The Greenville resident began to dominate at Delaware Park when the track opened in

1937. Lunger was best known nationally as the owner and breeder of Go For Wand, who was inducted into the Racing Hall of Fame in 1996. Go For Wand was voted the Eclipse Award winner in 1989 as the best two-year-old filly in the country when she won the 1989 Breeders' Cup Juvenile fillies in Florida. She won seven Grade I stakes before fatally breaking down in the 1990 Breeders' Cup Distaff at Belmont Park. "[Lunger] is the grand lady of Delaware racing," said William Rickman Jr., the president and CEO of Delaware Park. "Anybody who follows horse racing, especially in Delaware, knows the famed Christiana Stables. She is the most accomplished breeder and owner from Delaware and her legacy will live through the bloodlines of the horses she bred."

Lunger's Christiana Stables won four Delaware Handicaps (the most in track history) and three Delaware Oaks. Four major stakes at Delaware Park are named after fillies and mares she raced. There is the Grade III Endine Stakes, named after the 1958 and '59 DelCap winner Obeah, named after the DelCap champion (1969–70) and the Blue Hen winner in '67, and the Light Hearted Stakes, named after the winner of six straight races at Delaware, including the Delaware Oaks in 1972, and the dam of Go For Wand.

Other major stake winners at Delaware for Lunger include Camargo (1947 Delaware Oaks), Ricci Tavi (1956 Leonard Richards), Unity Hall (1970 Blue Hen), Plantain (1974 Delaware Oaks), Veiled Look (1981 Endine), Oh Say (1982 Hannibal, now known as the Damitrius) and Under the Rug (2000 Open Fire). Under the Rug ran second in 2008's Delaware Handicap. Three of Lunger's biggest grade one wins in New York came when Go For Wand won the 1990 Alabama and the Test and Thinking Cap won the 1955 Travers.[156]

Breeder and owner Bayard Sharp, an original director of Delaware Park and a former president of the Blood-Horse Inc., died on August 9, 2002, at his Centerville, Delaware home after a brief illness. He was eighty-nine. Sharp's career in racing spanned more than sixty years and involved racing thirty-nine stakes winners alone and in partnership, many of which were homebreds. He loved racing at Delaware because it was in his backyard, and also at Saratoga and in Florida. He was an owner who concentrated on breeding his horses rather than buying them at auction. He started with steeplechasers and also enjoyed fox hunting.

Sharp's first stakes winner, Speculate, captured the 1941 Grand National Steeplechase Handicap at Belmont Park and was steeplechase champion. Sharp's stable came to include flat runners. One of the good ones early on was Tide Rips, who won the 1948 Brandywine Handicap at Delaware Park and beat the mighty Stymie in winning that year's Monmouth Handicap. Sharp was one of several breeders and owners in Delaware and the surrounding area descending from DuPont patriarch E.I. DuPont. The others included Delaware Park founder William DuPont Jr. and Tide Rips's breeder, Marion DuPont Scott, plus Allaire DuPont of Kelso fame.

Born in Wilmington, Delaware, and a graduate of the University of Virginia, Sharp established his Sharp Farm near Middleton, Delaware, in 1941. The following year, while serving in the navy during World War II, he was relayed news that steeplechase rider Tom Roby had been involved in a crippling accident at Belmont. Sharp provided

Roby with funds for medical attention and later worked to see the inauguration of a race run in his honor. Sharp was admitted to the Jockey Club in 1952. At the time of his death, he was steward of that organization, plus an honorary trustee of the Blood-Horse Inc. and a trustee emeritus of the Thoroughbred Owners and Breeders Association.[157]

The park suffered another notable loss on January 26, 2004, with the death of John W. Rooney. Rooney helped lead Delaware Park through its most prosperous times and helped guide the track through the most trying times over his forty-four-year career. The native of Mahanoy City, Pennsylvania, started working at Delaware Park as the assistant treasurer for owner William DuPont Jr., President Donald P. Ross and general manager Byran Field in 1957, and had ascended to the position of vice-president of finance upon his retirement in 2001. In addition to serving as assistant treasurer and vice-president of finance, he was also the treasurer, finance controller, vice-president of racing and a steward at various times during his career at Delaware Park. He also worked for Delaware Park executives Donald P. Ross Jr., Baird Brittingham, Edward McLean, Austin Brown, John Mooney and William Fasy. In addition to all this, he also played an instrumental role in the transfer of track ownership to William Rickman in 1983.[158]

Track Records*

Main Track

Distance	Horse	Age	WGT	Date	Time
2 Furlongs	Glitter River	6	125	Sept. 5, 2000	:21.60
4½ Furlongs	Erlton	2	115	May 5, 1998	:51.80
5 Furlongs	Milky Way Gal	5	116	July 29, 1989	:56.20
5½ Furlongs	Trickle of Gold	4	119	May 6, 2006	1:02.68
6 Furlongs	Pisgah	5	123	April 25, 2006	1:07.92
1 Mile	Ashlar	4	117	June 25, 1960	1:35.20
1 Mile, 70 yards	Distinct Vision	3	115	Aug. 25, 2003	1:39.20
1 1/16 Miles	Lies of Omission	6	122	July 4, 1998	1:41.20
1⅛ Miles	Victoria Park	3	122	June 18, 1960	1:47.40
1 3/16 Miles	Gold Star Deputy	5	114	Oct. 31, 1999	1:56.72
1¼ Miles	Coup de Fusil	4	114	July 25, 1987	1:59.80
1½ Miles	Bam	5	115	June 26, 1948	2:31.00
1⅝ Miles	Flying Restina Run	5	121	Sept. 4, 2000	2:45.40
1¾ Miles	Cer Vantes	6	118	June 27, 1951	2:56.40
2 Miles	Dixies Act	5	118	Aug. 10, 1975	3:29.40
2 Miles, 70 yards	Wolfe Tone	6	114	Nov. 7, 1993	3:34.00
2¼ Miles	Sanguine Sword	8	114	July 2, 1986	3:58.60

Turf

Distance	Horse	Age	WGT	Date	Time
5 Furlongs	Mujado	4	116	July 27, 2002	:56.16
1 Mile	Hanover Hollywood	5	118	Aug. 3, 2002	1:34.74
1 1/16 Miles	Charablanc	5	108	July 20, 1963	1:40.20
1⅛ Miles	Foufa's Warrior	3	115	July 20, 2003	1:47.44
1⅜ Miles	Cool Prince	5	114	July 3, 1965	2:12.40
1½ Miles	Revved Up	5	116	July 20, 2003	2:26.46

TURF (CONTINUED)

Distance	Horse	Age	WGT	Date	Time
1 7/8 Miles	El Moro	8	116	July 22, 1963	3:11.80
2 Miles	Verdance	4	113	Sept. 21, 1986	3:24.40
2 3/8 Miles	Lively London	5	113	July 25, 1986	4:09.00
2 7/8 Miles	Call Louis	4	107	Aug. 24, 1986	5:08.20

STEEPLECHASE

Distance	Horse	Age	WGT	Date	Time
2 Miles	Devil's Path	5	152	July 21, 1978	3:49 2/5
2 1/4 Miles	Fabulous Time	8	154	July 2, 1982	4:12 3/5
Abt. 2 Miles	Balenchin	7	155	July 16, 1988	3:39 3/5
Abt. 2 1/4 Miles	Thrice Worthy	8	156	Sept. 22, 1984	4:13

*as of 2007

Notes

The Origins of American Horse Racing

1. Robertson, *Thoroughbred Racing in America*, 7.
2. Ibid., 18.
3. Ibid., 19.
4. Powell, 1928:278.
5. WPA, *Delaware*, 219.
6. Powell, *History of Delaware*, 178.
7. *Pennsylvania Packet*, October 15, 1778.

> *A PURSE of THREE HUNDRED DOLLARS to be run for on Wednesday the fourth day of November course near Christiana Bridge, Newcastle County, free for any horse, mare or gelding carrying age and blood agreeable to the rules of racing, the three mile heats; the horse winning two clear entitled to the purse. And on Thursday the fifth day of November, a purse of Fifty Pounds, free for any horse, mare or gelding, to the rules, &c. aforesaid, the winning horse the preceding day only excepted. And on Friday, the entrance money, free for scrubs only for the heats, once round the poles for the heat. Three reputed horses to start for the purses, or no race. Horses to be entered with JAMES GLENN, two days before the race, paying for the first purse Six Pounds, and for the second Three Pounds, or double at the post.—Proper persons to be appointed to settle all disputes that may arise. Vouchers for the blood and age of the horses to be produced if required.*

8. Robertson, *Thoroughbred Racing in America*, 31.
9. www.russpickett.com/history/claybio.htm.
10. Gelbert, *Great Delaware Sports Book*, 174.
11. Ibid., 175.
12. http://www.delawarestatefair.com/index.cfm?method=fairinfo.history.
13. History of Pimlico Race Course, in http://www.preakness.com.

Willie Built the Joint

14. *Time*, July 5, 1937.
15. Smith, "Paradise for Horse-Players."
16. *Time*, April 4, 1964.
17. International Tennis Federation, http://www.tennisfame.com.
18. *Wilmington Morning News*, January 1, 1966. See also 1947 biography and obit, *Newark Post*.
19. *Blood-Horse*, November 15, 2005.
20. Marion DuPont Scott Biography, http://emc.vetmed.vt.edu/emcmariondupontscott.html.

The Construction of Delaware Park

21. Smith, "Paradise for Horse-Players"; see also *Time*, October 8, 1928.
22. "Burke Heads New Track," *New York Times*, January 28, 1937. "Edward Burke, manager of the Havre de Grace, Md., race track, has been appointed manager of Delaware Park, under construction near Stanton, Del., by the Delaware Steeplechase and Race Association."
23. *New York Times*, January 2, 1947.
24. *Journal Every Evening*, June 24, 1937.
25. Ibid.
26. "Stanton Course Draws Leaders," *Newark Post*, June 17, 1937.
27. Smith, "Paradise for Horse-Players."
28. *Washington Post*, June 27, 1937.
29. *Journal Every Evening*, May 21, 1937.
30. Ibid., June 7, 1937.
31. Ibid., May 21, 1937.
32. Ibid., June 3, 1937.
33. Ibid., May 28, 1937.
34. Ibid., May 29, 1937.
35. Ibid., June 3, 1937.
36. *New York Times*, June 11, 1937.
37. Ibid., June 20, 1937.
38. *Journal Every Evening*, June 8, 1937.
39. Ibid.
40. Ibid., June 11, 1937.
41. Ibid., June 24, 1937.
42. Ibid.
43. Ibid.
44. Ibid.
45. Ibid., June 25, 1937.
46. *Wilmington Morning News*, June 26, 1937.
47. Ibid.
48. Ibid.

49. *Journal Every Evening*, June 25, 1937.
50. *Wilmington Morning News*, June 25, 1937.
51. *Journal Every Evening*, June 25, 1937.
52. "Man Behind Delaware Park," *Washington Post*, January 3, 1966.

Opening Day and Early Events

53. *New York Times*, June 26, 1937.
54. Smith, "Paradise for Horse-Players."

> *In the matter of irrigation, the shrubbery and running strip have it better than the patrons. Except in the private precincts of the Turf Club upstairs, no high-octane potables are sold, not even beer. Pioneers of the do-it-yourself fad, customers have been bringing their own in for twenty years. A race track without a bar is unusual, but not unique. Virtue was served similarly at Havre de Grace, in Maryland, possibly because a founding father of the Harford Agricultural and Breeders' Association, which operated that brindle path, was that pillar of rectitude and son of the Broadway soil, Mr. Arnold Rothstein, architect of the 1919 Black Sox scandal.*

55. "Delaware Park Divides Opening Feature Today," *Washington Post*, May 28, 1966.
56. *Time*, July 5, 1937.
57. *Journal Every Evening*, June 24, 1937.
58. *New York Times*, June 26, 1937.
59. *Wilmington Morning News*, March 25, 1937.
60. *Newark Post*, July 1, 1937.
61. *Journal Every Evening*, July 6, 1937.
62. Ibid., June 28, 1937.
63. Ibid., June 29, 1937.
64. Ibid., July 3, 1937.
65. Ibid., July 6, 1937.
66. *New York Times*, July 6, 1937.
67. *Journal Every Evening*, July 6, 1937.
68. Ibid.
69. *New York Times*, July 16, 1937.
70. *Newark Post*, August 6, 1937.
71. Ibid.
72. "$50,000 Expended for Additions to Course," *Newark Post*, June 2, 1938.
73. *Newark Post*, June 2, 1938.
74. *Time*, May 23, 1938.
75. Eddie Arcaro Biography, http://en.wikipedia.org/wiki/Eddie_Arcaro.
76. *New York Times*, June 14, 1940.

The War Years

77. *Washington Post*, May 25, 1941.

78. "Dobbin May Now Hail a Cab to Delaware Park," *Washington Post*, May 25, 1941.
79. *Time*, June 22, 1942.
80. *New York Times*, April 16, 1943.
81. *New York Times*, January 22, 1943. DuPont's statement was,

> *Public opinion will continue to dictate Delaware Park's policy. There is no profit to the stockholders to run a meeting and no loss to them if the track is closed down. It should not be lost sight of, however, that all connected with the track realize an obligation to the State and National Government to produce taxes. Also the horsemen should be thought of, and the public has indicated its interest in Delaware Park. Plans have been made to go on in 1943. They will be carried out unless wartime circumstances prevent.*

82. "Rene B. Takes Top Race at Delaware Park," *Washington Post*, June 1, 1941.
83. *New York Times*, March 7, 1944.
84. Smith, "Paradise for Horse-Players."
85. *New York Times*, June 7, 1944.

The Glory Years

86. http://en.wikipedia.org/wiki/Citation_(horse).
87. http://sports.si.cnn.com/default.asp?c=cnnsi&page=horse/kentucky/2007/history.htm.
88. "Delaware Park opens Tomorrow," *Washington Post*, May 28, 1951.
89. *Wilmington News Journal*, June 28, 1951.
90. Smith, "Paradise for Horse-Players."
91. *Blood-Horse*, March 26, 1955.
92. Smith, "Paradise for Horse-Players."

> *"How about making a play for the dolls?" Helen Stairwell suggested. She is Byran Field's assistant, daughter of a clergyman whose eyebrows did a flip when she went to work for a gambling house. "Dolls?" her boss said vaguely. "Females," she said, as to a child. "You know, Peachcakes, dames, fillies, twists, broads, if you'll pardon the expression. Somebody's-mother sort of thing." A light glittered in the general manager's eyes.*

93. Ibid.
94. *New York Times*, December 27, 1957.
95. Henry Clark, http://www.racingmuseum.org/hall/trainer.asp?ID=242.
96. *Wilmington News Journal*, May 29, 1959.
97. Ibid., May 30, 1959.
98. "Itobe Heads Field of 18 Sprinters," *Washington Post*, May 29, 1959.
99. "Japanese Horse Runs at Delaware," *Washington Post*, July 4, 1959.
100. *Wilmington News Journal*, June 19, 1960.
101. Silliman, *Time to Remember*, 110.
102. *Wilmington News Journal*, June 26, 1960.

The Story of Kelso

103. "Return to History: Oldest Living Kentucky Derby winner will be honored." http:www.kentuckyderbytours.com/htmls/oldest_jockey2.html.
104. *Wilmington News Journal*, May 13, 1999.
105. Gelbert, *Great Delaware Sports Book*, 181.
106. *New York Times*, June 11, 1965.
107. http://horseracing.about.com/od/ famoushorses/a/aa070598_2.htm.
108. Gelbert, *Great Delaware Sports Book*, 181.
109. *Messenger* 2, no. 1 (Fall 1992): 3.

The Park During the 1960s and 1970s

110. *Wilmington News Journal*, June 29, 1964.
111. *New York Times*, June 28, 1964.
112. "Delaware Park Sets $4 Million Modernization," *Washington Post*, February 16, 1969.
113. *New York Times*, February 16, 1969.
114. *Washington Post*, May 28, 1970.
115. *New York Times*, October 27, 1991.
116. "Jane DuPont Lunger, Who Raced Go For Broke, Dies," *Blood Horse*, September 19, 2001.
117. Willie Shoemaker, http://en.wikipedia.org/wiki/Willie_Shoemaker.
118. *New York Times*, February 22, 1971.
119. *Wilmington News Journal*, April 2, 1975.

Tragedies at the Park

120. *New York Times*, June 5, 1950.
121. Ibid., June 3, 1959; *Wilmington News Journal*, June 3, 1959.
122. *Wilmington News Journal*, June 11, 1965.
123. *New York Times*, March 8, 1968.
124. *Wilmington News Journal*, November 6, 1999.
125. Ibid., March 25, 2000.

Death, Resurrection and a Horse We All Loved

126. *New York Times*, September 30, 1982.
127. "What's Going on Here?" *Blood Horse*, October 9, 1982, 6837.
128. "Delaware Park Reported Sold to Pair from Maryland," *Philadelphia Inquirer*, August 28, 1983.
129. "New Owners Christmas, Rickman plan host of changes at Delaware Park," *Philadelphia Inquirer*, August 29, 1983.
130. *Puerto Rico Herald*, July 6, 2001.
131. *New York Times*, July 29, 1987.
132. *Wilmington News Journal*, September 28, 1995
133. *Wilmington News Journal*, September 30, 1995.

134. Ibid., June 4, 1996.
135. *Wilmington News Journal*, February 6, 1999.
136. Ibid., March 26, 2000.
137. Ibid., April 7, 2000.
138. Ibid., February 23, 2002.
139. "At Delaware Park, a Disappointed Swarm," *Philadelphia Inquirer*, May 8, 2005.
140. http://en.wikipedia.org/wiki/Alex's_Lemonade_Stand.
141. *Blood-Horse*, October 2, 2005.
142. "Barbaro's Battle to Survive Still Inspires," http://www.msnbc.msn.com/id/15063293.
143. *Baltimore Sun*, November 20, 2006.
144. *Wilmington News Journal*, January 30, 2007.
145. "Barbaro's birthday celebrated at Delaware Park," *Thoroughbred Times*, April 29, 2007.
146. *The Horse*, March 5, 2007.
147. *Wilmington News Journal*, September 19, 2006.
148. "Delaware Panel Issues Steroids Ban," *Blood-Horse*, December 14, 2007.
149. http://www.delawarepark.com/about_history.php
150. http://www.delawarepark.com/about_history.php
151. *Wilmington News Journal*, July 26, 1999.

FONDLY REMEMBERED

152. *New York Times*, January 2, 1947.
153. "Delaware Park Official Dies," *Washington Post*, June 25, 1965.
154. *New York Times*, October 12, 1973.
155. Obituary of Donald P. Ross, *Wilmington News Journal*, July 4, 2000.
156. *Wilmington News Journal*, September 20, 2001.
157. *Blood-Horse*, August 12, 2002.
158. *Wilmington News Journal*, January 28, 2004.

References Cited

Baltimore Sun.

Blood-Horse.

Gelbert, Doug. *The Great Delaware Sports Book.* Montchanin, DE: Manatee Books, 1995.

Halpin, Warren T. *Hoof Beats: Drawings and Comments by Warren T. Halpin.* Introductions on polo by Stewart B. Iglehart, hunting by Henry G. Vaughan and steeplechase by William DuPont Jr. Philadelphia: J.B. Lippincott, 1938.

Journal Every Evening (Wilmington, DE).

Newark (DE) Post.

News Journal (Wilmington, DE).

New York Times.

Page, R. Brian. *Delaware in the Great Depression.* Charleston, SC: Arcadia, 2005.

Pennsylvania Packet (Philadelphia).

Philadelphia Inquirer.

Powell, Walter A. *A History of Delaware.* Boston: Christopher Publishing House, 1928.

Reed, Henry C. *Delaware, A History of the First State.* New York: Lewis Historical Publishing Company, 1947.

Robertson, William H.P. *History of Thoroughbred Racing in America.* New York: Bonanza Books, 1964.

Silliman, Charles A. *A Time to Remember.* Privately printed, Wilmington, 1962.

Smith, Red. "Paradise for Horse-Players: A Unique Approach to racing is found at the Delaware Park Track, a millionaire's pet project, where the customers are pampered and profit is no object." *Saturday Evening Post,* June 1957.

Thoroughbred Times.

Time.

Washington Post.

Wilmington (DE) Morning News.

Works Progress Administration. *Delaware, Guide to the First State.* New York: Heritage House, 1938.

About the Author

Ken Baumgardt is a professional historian who was employed in the field of cultural resource management for more than twenty-five years. Born and raised in Newark, Delaware, his family home was within a half-mile of Delaware Park. He attended local schools and graduated from the University of Delaware in 1982 with a bachelor of arts in history, with an emphasis on American studies.

Mr. Baumgardt comes from a long line of prominent scholars and educators. Several noted writers are close relatives, including Samuel Kercheval, author of *A History of the Valley of Virginia* (1833); Zane Grey (January 31, 1872–October 23, 1939), author of more than ninety works that popularized an image of the Old West; and Margaret Mitchell (November 8, 1900–August 16, 1949), 1939 Pulitzer Prize winner for her epic novel, *Gone with the Wind*.

He was a field archaeologist and historian for the cultural resource management firm of MAAR Associates in Newark, Delaware, from 1980 to 1991, and in that year was hired by the U.S. Army Corps of Engineers, Baltimore District, as a cultural resources manager, a position he continues to hold. While with MAAR Associates, he was responsible for researching and documenting historical and archaeological resources throughout the middle Atlantic region, and also had the opportunity to do research in the U.S. Virgin Islands; Beersheva, Israel; and Niamey, Niger, Africa. In addition to his regular work, Baumgardt is also on the Baltimore District Emergency First Responder Team, and served in disaster response for Hurricanes Katrina, Rita and others.

He currently resides in the colonial village of Christiana, Delaware, and is active in supporting the historic and cultural activities that benefit the community. Proceeds from this book will be used to continue to conduct research and writing on local topics of interest. He also has a large collection of memorabilia associated with the town, and hopes to establish a local history museum there.